Words of Life

**THE BIBLE DAY BY DAY
WITH THE SALVATION ARMY**

PENTECOST EDITION MAY-AUGUST 2001

Hodder & Stoughton
LONDON SYDNEY AUCKLAND

AND THE SALVATION ARMY

Copyright © 2001 by The Salvation Army

First published in Great Britain in 2001

The right of The Salvation Army to be identified as the
Author of the Work has been asserted by them in accordance with the
Copyright, Designs and Patents Act 1988.

10 9 8 7 6 5 4 3 2 1

All rights reserved. No part of this publication may be reproduced, stored in a
retrieval system, or transmitted, in any form or by any means without the prior
written permission of the publisher, nor be otherwise circulated in any form of
binding or cover other than that in which it is published and without a similar
condition being imposed on the subsequent purchaser.

British Library Cataloguing in Publication Data
A record for this book is available from the British Library

ISBN 0 340 75700 0

Printed and bound in Great Britain by
Omnia Books

Hodder & Stoughton
A Division of Hodder Headline Ltd
338 Euston Road
London NW1 3BH

WHO ARE YOU, GOD?

Moses-like
I stand before an autumn tree
and ask, 'Who are you, God?'

The old names have been beautiful
like leaves that carried the seasons through.
They cradled me with gentle arms when I was young,
they beamed their approval over my growing years,
they gave me shelter in my teens
when sadness and loss howled their storms around me.

Now in an autumned life, I need to let them fall.
It's painful to let them go,
like walking away from lifelong friends
but like autumn leaves they fall to make way for new growth.
In the place where they come to rest
a rich, fragrant mulch will form,
nurturing my tree and giving vigour to spring's growth.

So help me to let them go, Lord, one by one
and in their place to welcome
new names I have never called you before,
lifelong familiar, but unexpressed.

> Extravagant God
> Intimate Friend
> Artist of crazy colour and beauty
> Song-giver
> Companion on my journey

These new names beckon me on
into a new dance
a new season
a new beginning.
And in naming you afresh
I hear you whisper my own new name.
Like Moses, I take off my shoes.
This too is holy ground.

Barbara Sampson

CONTENTS

Major Barbara Sampson writes...

New Beginnings
1–5 May

Who is God?
7–26 May

Pentecost Meditations
(Colonel Earl Robinson)
27 May–10 June

Letter of 1 John
11–23 June

Mark's Gospel 1–3
25 June–21 July

Proverbs in Person
23–28 July

Called to be the People of God
30 July–18 August

Lord, Teach Us to Pray
20–31 August

SUNDAYS
Psalms 1–14

MAJOR BARBARA SAMPSON WRITES...

In my twenty-five years of Salvation Army officership, few appointments have been as daunting as this one. In taking over from Commissioner Harry Read as author of *Words of Life*, I realise that I am stepping into very large footprints.

So often have I felt like that little boy of John 6 who offered his meagre lunch to Jesus, and then watched a miracle taking place. In Jesus' hands, five loaves and two fish became a nourishing and more-than-adequate meal for a hungry multitude.

Could it be that in Jesus' hands, the crumbs of my reflections could become nourishment for a hungry world? I have written each day under the blessing of God's promise:

> 'The Sovereign Lord has given me an instructed tongue,
> to know the word that sustains the weary.
> He wakens me morning by morning,
> wakens my ear to listen like one being taught'
>
> *Isaiah 54:5*

My greatest joy will be to know that these daily readings have indeed been a means of sustenance and blessing to you, the reader. May God bless us through these months as we journey together.

ABBREVIATIONS USED

AV   Authorised (King James) Version
NIV   New International Version
NRSV   New Revised Standard Version

SASB   *The Song Book of The Salvation Army*, 1986

TUESDAY 1 MAY

A New Song

Psalm 40

'He put a new song in my mouth, a hymn of praise to our God' (v. 3, NIV).

It's 1 May – a day of new beginnings. This is the beginning of a new month, a new edition of *Words of Life* and, among other things, the start of the duck-shooting season here in New Zealand. From today on, the population of protected duck ponds will dramatically increase with ducks seeking refuge. Every morning will be roll-call time!

As the new author of *Words of Life*, I greet you, the reader. I have had you in mind as I have written these daily notes, but the picture at times has been rather blurry. Are you young or old, a busy person or with time on your hands, living in the northern hemisphere and enjoying the surprises of spring, or living in the southern hemisphere and feeling a cool slide into winter? Do you like deep theological debate, or something practical to help you live your Christian life more meaningfully? I have no way of answering these questions, so have had to trust God to give me a word every day that would bless you.

There is an old Christian tradition that God sends each person into the world with a special message to deliver,

with a special song to sing for others,

with a special act of love to bestow.

No one else can speak my message, or sing my song, or offer my act of love, for these are entrusted only to me.

I have been a Salvation Army officer for twenty-six years and have served in corps (parish) and training appointments in my home country of New Zealand, and at Chikankata Secondary School in Zambia. I have two adult children, a daughter-in-law and four energetic young grandsons. I delight to live in the land of the All Blacks, the flightless kiwi, mountains second only to Switzerland's in magnificence, four million people and fifty million sheep.

In an activist Army, I've discovered that I'm a contemplative. Here in *Words of Life*, I offer to you the God-given fruits of that contemplation. This is my message, my new song, my act of love.

WEDNESDAY 2 MAY
A New Creation

Revelation 21:1–7

'I am making everything new!' (v. 5, NIV).

On a recent holiday, my husband, daughter and I stayed at a house that was undergoing major renovation. The owners had already done up a couple of rooms (in garish colours, I might add), but they had obviously decided to speed up the process by tackling the rest of the house all at once, rather than room by room.

Everywhere inside was chaotic with broken windows, partly dismantled walls and cupboards, and temporary fixtures. The place was a 'messy's' paradise, but being a man who likes everything neat and tidy, my husband found it simply horrible.

And yet, there was something more. The owners had obviously seen great potential and even beauty in the place, and they were on a mission to restore it to its former glory. The solid timber floors had been scraped bare and would eventually be polished. Lead-light windows which were now cracked or broken would one day shine again. New paint would work wonders! The dream for it all was held in the heart of the owners, and they were getting there, one step at a time.

Isn't it true that, as Christians, we live in a house that is undergoing long-term, even constant renovation? We are being transformed from the inside. It's not a matter of being rebuilt to a former glory, but rather to a new glory. God's way of working this inner transformation may often feel messy and even chaotic but, somehow, a master craftsman is at work, following a design that he has had in his heart for a long, long time. We may not always like his choice of décor or taste in colour, his means of making the transformation happen. But God sees the end from the beginning, the potential for grace and glory that lies within us, and so he presses on, one step at a time.

To reflect on
A friend who has recently become a Christian was asked, 'How do you know that Jesus is alive today?' Her immediate response, 'Because of the difference he is making in my life.' That's a testimony to transformation!

THURSDAY 3 MAY
A New Community

Galatians 3:26–4:7

'In Christ's family there can be no division into Jew and non-Jew, slave and free, male and female. Among us you are all equal. That is, we are all in a common relationship with Jesus Christ' (v. 28, *The Message*).

In the mid-1970s, fresh from our commissioning as Salvation Army officers, my husband and I, with our two small children, went to our first appointment, Chikankata Secondary School, Zambia. My husband taught on the school staff while I did some secretarial work and childcare that fitted in with the needs of our family.

In the holidays, Bible schools were often held at the secondary school, or at an outlying village centre. Local corps leaders would come for a week of intensive study. At one Bible school my husband and I and a colleague formed the teaching team with a large group of very enthusiastic students. These were people hungry to learn new Bible truths, so that they could go home and feed their own people.

For the whole week, we studied 2 Corinthians 5:17: 'If anyone is in Christ, he is a new creation; the old has gone, the new has come!' It was like holding a diamond up to the light as we studied this verse from all angles.

On the Thursday morning I introduced the topic of 'the new community' into which we are called as believers. This community has no barriers of race, gender, age or experience, and no entry qualifications other than faith in Christ. As I spoke, the class was still, the people obviously moved to hear such a message. And as it impacted on them, it hit me also. Here I was, out in the Zambian bush, thousands of miles from my home country, among a people whose skin colour, background and opportunities were all different from mine, and yet we were brothers and sisters in a family together, because we were all children of God! The things we held in common were greater and more numerous than all the things that would separate us, label us as 'different' from each other, or set us apart.

The memory of that morning still hits me, twenty-five years later!

To reflect on
Today, greet another believer as your brother or sister in Christ.

FRIDAY 4 MAY
A New Beauty

2 Corinthians 5:16–21

'If anyone is in Christ, he is a new creation; the old has gone, the new has come' (v. 17, NIV).

Recently a friend took me on a walking expedition to a quarry on the outskirts of Christchurch. The quarry was opened in the late 1850s and, for just on 140 years, it provided fine blue-grey stone for many stately buildings in the Christchurch area and beyond. In 1990 it closed down, being of no further use. It was just a blot on the landscape, a great gaping scar. But over the past few years it has gradually been transformed into a place of leisure.

A well-formed walking track passes by the old stone-crushing plant and quarry buildings up to a number of viewing points on the quarry rim. At each viewing platform there is an information board telling the history of the quarry and the method by which the stone was processed. Interpretation panels explain the different rock forms that can be seen. The top viewing platform gives spectacular views over the Canterbury Plains to Lake Ellesmere and the Southern Alps. Newly planted areas of native trees and shrubs and a grove of walnut trees lead down to a gully where a spacious picnic area has been set up. The old stone cottage, built in 1922, that once housed the single men workers is now being redeveloped as an information centre.

The whole quarry is beautiful in an ugly kind of way. The jagged rock formations with their range of soft colours serve no practical purpose now, other than inviting people into a piece of local history, and offering a place for leisure and recreation.

How like God, who delights in taking ugly things and making them beautiful! The cross would be the supreme example of God doing that – taking something ugly and transforming it into the most wonderful symbol of our faith. Thank God that he is still in the transforming business today!

To sing
Something beautiful, something good,
All my confusion he understood.
All I had to offer him was brokenness and strife,
But he made something beautiful out of my life.

(Bill Gaither)[1]

SATURDAY 5 MAY
A New Command

John 13:31–38

'A new command I give you: Love one another. As I have loved you, so you must love one another. By this all men will know that you are my disciples, if you love one another' (vv. 34, 35, NIV).

When my son was in his early teens and eating as if every meal was his last, he used to try out his developing muscles on his mother! If I retaliated, he would increase his force until I called a halt to the game. 'You might as well face it, Mum,' he said one day, 'whatever you do to me, I'll do twice as hard back to you.' In a moment of inspiration, I replied, 'Then I'll love you.'

We live in a world where the so-called right to retaliate spills over in families, communities and even nations, with tragic consequences. 'You touch my car, and I'll rearrange your face' is, sadly, much more than a bumper sticker.

Jesus calls believers, however, to a radically different response. 'Has someone pushed you round a bit?' he asks. 'Then don't keep score, keep silent. Don't get even, get prayerful, get forgiving, get loving!' Of course such a response is not natural, but supernatural. Only God can give us the strength to respond like that.

When Jesus spoke his command to his disciples, he had just recently washed their feet and was preparing to die for them. This command was one of his last words to them, the summary of three years of teaching. 'You might forget all that I've said, but don't forget this – love one another, just as I have loved you.'

This instruction, as old as Leviticus 19:18, is still God's new command to us today. Churches, Army corps and Bible-study home groups are all called to be fellowships of Christly love. Such groups, living out the command to love, will nurture and bless those who belong and, like a glowing light on a dark night, will attract others. The prophet Zechariah spoke of people who would grab a Jewish man's robe and say, 'Let us go with you, because we have heard that God is with you' (*Zech 8:23*).

To reflect on
'Look how these people love one another.' Can this be said of your fellowship?

SUNDAY 6 MAY
Make Me Like a Tree

Psalm 1

'Blessed is the man . . . his delight is in the law of the LORD,
and on his law he meditates day and night' (vv. 1,2, NIV).

Psalm 1 stands as an entrance-way into the book of Psalms. We come to it from a world of push and shove, ceaseless movement and activity. Psalm 1 helps us as we leave the world of noise and enter into a world of mystery and wonder. The first word, 'blessed', sets the tone, arousing our expectation and readiness for the gracious gifts God has for us.

Psalm 1 contains an action and an image. *Torah*-meditation is the action; a transplanted tree is the image. The noun *torah* is from a verb that means 'to throw something, such as a javelin, so that it hits its mark'. In living speech, words are javelins that are hurled from one mind into another. God's word has such an aimed, intentional nature. When he speaks to us, his words get inside us and work their meaning.

Isaiah used this word 'meditate' for the sounds that a lion makes over its prey (*Isa 31:4*) as he growls in pleasure. We are to do more than merely read God's words. This psalm invites us to take them in, chew them over, and let the sounds sink into the depths of our being. When we do that, we are like a tree, planted by streams of water.

At the time that the psalms were collected, the people of Israel were in exile in Babylon. In that strange and ungodly land, they felt cut off from their home and from their God. They thought they couldn't pray (see *Ps 137*). But they did, by immersing themselves in meditation. Like trees, planted along the banks of the irrigation ditches in that foreign land, they too put down roots.

The contrast between the godly (those who delight in and meditate continually on God's words) and the wicked (those who don't) is striking. The godly are like trees, fruitful, lush, evergreen. The wicked are like chaff, without substance, blown away by the wind.

Today as you come to prayer, go, find yourself a tree, sit down in front of it and look at it long and thoughtfully!

WHO IS GOD?

Introduction

<u>Psalm 113</u>

'Let the name of the LORD be praised, both now and for evermore' (v. 2, NIV).

At the beginning of the book of Exodus, Moses is chosen, called and set apart by God to deliver the children of Israel from the oppressive rule of the Egyptians. In commissioning Moses for this daunting task, God assures him of his presence. Moses asks what name he is to use to refer to God and is told, 'I AM WHO I AM ... The LORD, the God of your fathers – the God of Abraham, the God of Isaac and the God of Jacob ... This is my name for ever' (*Exod 3:14,15*).

Who are you, God? What is your name? What name do I call you? Such questions do not belong solely to a great leader like Moses. They are questions that belong to every seeker after truth, every believer who wants to follow God in a growing intimacy of relationship. Knowing his name means knowing his character.

From the earliest chapters of the Old Testament, the names of God open up a gradually unfolding revelation of himself. He is:

Jehovah, the Eternal Lord
El-Elyon, God Most High
Adonai, Sovereign Master; and he is also:
Jehovah-Shalom, the Lord is Peace
Jehovah-Rophi, the Lord Our Healer
Jehovah-Rohi, the Lord Our Shepherd, and many more.

Each new name reveals something more of God's character and nature, like a great multidimensional mosaic being uncovered.

For the next three weeks, this series on the names of God explores some of the pieces of that mosaic. May our understanding of who God is grow as a result of these reflections, and may we discover, in greater measure, that the name of God is indeed 'a strong tower' (*Prov 18:10*), a place of safety and refuge for the righteous.

MONDAY 7 MAY
Elohim – God

Genesis 17:1–8

'In the beginning God . . .' (Gen 1:1, NIV).

Elohim, the great name of God, is written like the author's signature at the very beginning of the Genesis account. The opening chapter of the book of Genesis introduces the two main subjects of Holy Scripture – God the Creator and man his creature, and sets the scene for the long story of their relationship. The opening verses are like a great hymn of praise, not unlike some of the psalms, which dramatically sets out the omnipotence of the Creator. The God of Abraham, Isaac and Jacob is not merely a local deity, nor some tribal chieftain, but the sovereign Lord of the whole earth.

This God who speaks the world into being and creates order by his very word of command is called *Elohim*. In the first two chapters of Genesis, *Elohim* occurs thirty-five times in connection with God's creative power. The word is in the plural, e.g. 'God [plural] said, "Let us [plural] make man in our image" ' (*Gen 1:26*). This is the 'plural of majesty', a God who is one, but made up of the three members of the Trinity – Father, Son and Holy Spirit.

Elohim, used as the name of God, implies fullness of might, and speaks of one who stands in a covenant relationship with his people for the fulfilment of his purposes. In Genesis 17:1–8, when God appears to Abram and pledges himself in covenant relationship with him and his descendants, he says he will be their *Elohim*. This pledge at the heart of God's covenant promise is repeated over and over again in the Old Testament. Using his own name, God promises that he will be the protector of his people, and the guarantor of their future blessing.

Reflection today on this name of God reminds us that the God who set the universe in motion is still faithful in keeping his promises and the covenant relationship with his people.

To reflect on

Today, as God lovingly reminds you, 'I will be to you "Elohim" ', may your response be 'My Elohim, in whom I trust' (Ps 91:2).

TUESDAY 8 MAY
Jahweh (Jehovah) – Eternal Lord

Exodus 3:1–15

'God said to Moses, "I AM WHO I AM. This is what you are to say to the Israelites: 'I AM has sent me to you' " ' (v. 14, NIV).

The name of God which is the most precious to Jewish people, and most revealing of his grace, is the name *Jehovah*. It occurs about seven thousand times in the Old Testament. This name was held in such reverence that it was whispered only by the high priest in the Holy of Holies once a year, and even today Jews refrain from writing it or pronouncing it.

Rabbinical writings refer to it as 'the Great and Terrible Name', 'the Incommunicable Name', 'the Holy Name'. It was also known as 'the Name of Four Letters' because it was originally composed of four consonants, YHWH, to which the vowels of *Adonai* were added, making it *Jehovah*, with the original pronunciation *Yahweh*.

This name is derived from the Hebrew verb *havah* meaning 'to be' or 'being'. While it is translated 'Lord', its meaning is more fully 'He that always was, that always is, and ever is to come'. When Moses asked for God's name, and he replied 'I AM WHO I AM', he was expressing his own self-existence, unchangeableness and permanence. From infinity in the past, to infinity in the future, he is and will be God.

Further, *Jehovah* is God's name of covenant relationship. He is not only the everlasting one, the same yesterday, today and for ever, but he is also the ever-loving one, who has brought grace and salvation from their origin in an eternal past, to their fulfilment in this present moment, to their perfect goal in an eternal future.

Just as the sun spreads its rays of light to all the corners of the world, so this name *Jehovah* with its various descriptions shines forth to give believers a true and fuller picture of the being and glory of God. So he is *Jehovah* – Lord, *Jehovah-Elohim* – the Majestic, Omnipotent God, *Jehovah-Elohay* – the Lord My God, *Jehovah-Gmolah* – the God of Recompense.

These names and others will provide a rich feast of reflection for us in the next few days.

To reflect on
'This name Jehovah is God's memorial, God's forget-me-not'.
(H. E. Govan)

WEDNESDAY 9 MAY
El-Elyon – God Most High

Genesis 14:13–24

'For you, O LORD, are the Most High over all the earth; you are exalted far above all gods' (Psalm 97:9, NIV).

The name *El-Elyon*, God Most High, is first introduced in *Genesis 14*. Abram's blessed and tranquil life in Canaan had been disrupted by an invasion led by Kedorlaomer, king of Elam. For twelve years the cities of the Dead Sea plain submitted and then they rebelled. Kedorlaomer reacted swiftly and reconquered them. When he defeated Sodom, he captured Lot, his family and his possessions (*v. 12*).

This led to Abram's intervention. With only 318 men and God's help, he chased Kedorlaomer's army, attacked and defeated them and recovered his nephew Lot and his family. On his return, Abram was met near Salem (probably Jerusalem) by Melchizedek, its priest-king, and by the king of Sodom. Melchizedek greets Abram warmly, offering food and drink as a sign of friendship and hospitality. Then he blesses Abram in the name of *El-Elyon*, God Most High. In blessing Abram, Melchizedek is himself blessed. Abram responds by giving him a tenth of the booty he has taken (*v. 20*).

In contrast, the ungodly king of Sodom is disdainful. Abram refuses to take any booty from him, as he does not want to give this king any excuse for claiming that he had made Abram rich. The king of Sodom will find out that it is dangerous to despise those whom God blesses.

In this account, Abram is shown to be far more than a wandering Bedouin with a few herds and slaves. He is now a man of wealth, substance and standing. Above all, he is a man living under the blessing of God. For those with eyes to see, such as Melchizedek, *El-Elyon*, the God Most High, is with Abram. God's promise to make Abram's name great and for him to be a blessing has begun to be fulfilled. With God on his side, Abram is generous, and passes the blessings on to others.

To reflect on
Above every other name that is great and powerful stands the name of El-Elyon, God Most High. Lift your heart to his greatness today.

THURSDAY 10 MAY
El-Roi – God Who Sees

Genesis 16:1–16

'I have now seen the One who sees me' (v. 13, NIV).

The characters
- Sarah (elderly, rich and powerful, childless and ashamed, impatient with God)
- Hagar (a foreign slave girl)
- Abram (elderly, the master, content to wait on God's timing, but also under the control of Sarah)

The problem
- Hagar becomes pregnant to Abram
- Hagar looks down on Sarah
- Sarah blames Abram
- Abram shrugs his shoulders
- Sarah abuses Hagar
- Hagar runs away

The resolution
- God speaks to Hagar
- Hagar returns to Abram
- Ishmael is born
- Abram loves Ishmael
- Sarah unavailable for comment!

This biblical account sounds like a modern-day TV soap opera. If Hagar had been able to take Sarah to court for abusing her, or bring a charge against Abram for his weak-handed part in the affair, the story would have hit the headlines. But Hagar had no court to appeal to, and was forced to take her only way out, which was to run away.

Alone in the wilderness, she is sitting by a spring of water when she is found by an angel of the Lord. Gradually she realises that he is a messenger from God. He orders her to return to her mistress in humility, and promises that from her will come descendants beyond counting. As the angel disappears, Hagar gives the Lord a new name – *El-Roi* – God who sees me (and who looks after me). In her extremity of need, the God who sees grants to Hagar an experience of grace. The water beside which she had been sitting when God found her is likewise named *Beer Lahai Roi* – 'the well of the living one who sees me', or 'the well of continuing to live after seeing God' (*v. 14; cf. Gen 32:30*).

To reflect on
Today, call on **El–Roi – *God who sees you (and who looks after you).***

FRIDAY 11 MAY
El-Olam – The Everlasting God

Genesis 21:22–34

'Abraham . . . called upon the name of the LORD, the Eternal God'
(v. 33, NIV).

The story of Abraham's treaty with Abimelech at Beersheba gives a glimpse into the quiet pastoral and family life of Abraham, Sarah and young Isaac. King Abimelech and his commander Phicol have recognised that Abraham has become a blessing in the land, and they want to ensure on-going peace and harmony with his descendants by making a long-term non-aggression treaty. Abraham agrees but complains about a well of water that Abimelech's servants had taken from him. The two men sort the matter out, a treaty is made, and the place is named Beersheba, 'well of the oath', as a permanent reminder of their agreement.

In gratitude to God for his continued faithfulness, Abraham plants a tamarisk tree and worships God, calling him *El-Olam* – everlasting, eternal God. The name speaks of God who is without a beginning, who will never cease to be, who will never grow old, and to whom the present moment is just a tiny piece of eternity. In that name, Abraham was affirming what the psalmist would later declare, 'From everlasting to everlasting you are God' (*Ps 90:2*).

I recall as a child being fascinated by a description of eternity as a bird flying past a huge iron ball once every hundred years, and gently sweeping her wing across the ball. Eternity would be the time it would take for the iron ball to be worn away by the touch of the bird's wing.

With his own supply of life-giving water, Abraham is reassured about his future and God's continued provision for his needs. Peace and stability settle around him. He wears tranquil old age like a cloak of God's blessing. What could possibly go wrong now with so much going right? Abraham is not to know that this is merely the lull before the storm.

To reflect on
The eternal, everlasting God, El-Olam, is the God who never grows tired or weary, and who renews the strength of those who hope in him (see Isa 40:28–31).

SATURDAY 12 MAY

Jehovah-Jireh – The God Who Provides

Genesis 22:1–19

'So Abraham called that place The LORD Will Provide' (v. 14, NIV).

Jehovah-Jireh is used in Scripture only once, and then as the name of a place. Abraham, over 100 years old, had come to the contented eventide of his life. The testing of his faith concerning the birth of a son had given way to joy in the gift of Isaac. He was at peace in the land, neighbourly disputes had been settled, his flocks and herds were abundant.

Suddenly, in the midst of this tranquil life came a command from God; a startling, terrible, incomprehensible command to take Isaac to Moriah and offer him there in sacrifice. This son of promise, for whom he had waited for twenty-five years, was dearer than life itself, but Abraham's devotion to God meant he could only obey.

Getting up early, he gathered the servants and the boy, saddled the donkey, cut the wood for the sacrifice, and set out. They trudged for three days to Moriah, then Abraham and the boy went on alone. How anguished the thoughts of this 'friend of God' must have been as he staggered forward. Isaac broke the silence, asking about a lamb for the sacrifice. Abraham replied: 'God himself will provide the lamb.'

Reaching the designated place, Abraham built the altar for the sacrifice, tied up the boy and was ready to slit his throat, when an angel called insistently from heaven, 'Abraham! Abraham!' The previous command, 'Go and sacrifice your son' (v. 2), is now changed to 'Do not lay a hand on the boy' (v. 12). Abraham has passed the test. Isaac is released. A ram caught by his horns in a thicket becomes the sacrifice in his place. Does Abraham do a dance of thanksgiving, or collapse in sheer exhaustion and relief? To commemorate the divine intervention, he names the place *Jehovah-Jireh*: 'The Lord will see to it. He will provide.'

Isaac asked, 'Where is the lamb?' Two thousand years later, John the Baptist answers that very question as he points to Jesus and says, 'Behold the Lamb of God!' (*John 1:36, AV*).

To reflect on
Abraham's total trust is matched by God's total provision.

SUNDAY 13 MAY
God is Laughing!

Psalm 2

'The One enthroned in heaven laughs; the Lord scoffs at them'
(v. 4, NIV).

Psalm 2 is the second half of a two-part introduction to the Psalms, proclaiming the blessedness of all who acknowledge the Lordship of God and his Anointed One, and who 'take refuge in him' (v. 12). This psalm is frequently quoted in the New Testament, where it is applied to Christ as the great Son of David and God's Anointed (see *Acts 4:25,26; 13:33; Heb 1:5,6*).

Psalm 2 has a dramatic quality to it. We hear first the voice of the nations in defiance (vv. 1–3). Instead of rejoicing in God's blessings, the nations are rebelling against God's rule. They want to be free! The picture is of a wild and rebellious animal that wants to break the chain that restrains him. The rebellion of the nations is against God, and his Anointed One (Jesus). But God calls their effort a 'vain' thing, because he knows that it is impossible to have true freedom apart from submission to holy authority.

God's voice sounds forth in derision (vv. 4–6). The nations of the earth are raging like beasts, shaking their fists against heaven, but God is laughing. Almighty God ridicules the attacks, for he maintains his authority whether people accept his rule or not.

The voice of the Son speaks next (vv. 7–9). God may give people freedom even to rebel, but human rebellion can never overthrow God's purposes. Even when the people crucified Christ, they unconsciously fulfilled 'God's set purpose and foreknowledge' (*Acts 2:23*).

Jesus Christ is not only the Son of God and the reigning King, but he is also the Judge. One day he will return and smash the nations to pieces the way a potter smashes useless pottery. And so God appeals to people to stop rebelling (vv. 10–12). 'Be wise,' he calls. 'Serve the LORD with fear.' 'Kiss the Son!' It is our call today as well, that we submit to the Lord, hail him as King, and accept him as the God of grace before he comes as God the Judge.

Pray today for the rulers of the earth, that they will 'kiss the Son'.

MONDAY 14 MAY

Jehovah-Zimrath – The Lord is My Song

Exodus 15:1–21

'The LORD is my strength and my song; he has become my salvation' (v. 2, NIV).

The song of Moses and Miriam in Exodus 15 is considered to be the oldest recorded song in the world. It is a festive epic poem, a great song of praise for God's victory. The song is about God and to God. He has risen to the crisis of his people's apparently hopeless cause. Fleeing from Egypt, they are trapped, Pharaoh's army in pursuit, the deep waters of the Red Sea ahead.

Pharaoh's army offers no threat to God. Their boastfulness, 'I will pursue, I will overtake, I will divide, I will gorge myself, I will draw my sword' (v. 9) is futile. God blows with his wind, and they sink like lead into the mighty waters. In this conflict with the children of Israel and God on one side, and all the military might of Egypt on the other, God has won, decisively, gloriously, unforgettably. Forget they will not! He is praised as *Jehovah-Zimrath* – the Lord is my Song.

At times, God gives us a song to sing, not after a victory, but in the midst of the conflict. It was so for a Chinese pastor who was imprisoned for eighteen years for his faith. In the harsh labour camp, his task was to empty the cesspool, into which all the human waste from the camp was poured. The pit was so large and deep that he had to wade right into it, scooping out successive layers of the disease-ridden mass. The guards and other prisoners kept well away, because of the stench.

'But I liked working there,' he said, 'because I was alone and could pray and sing to the Lord as loudly as I wanted to. My favourite song took on new meaning for me in that place: *I come to the garden alone, while the dew is still on the roses* . . . As I sang that hymn, again and again, I knew the Lord was with me. In that private garden, the Lord became my song and my salvation.'

To reflect on
What song do you sing to the Lord today?

TUESDAY 15 MAY
Jehovah-Rophi – The Lord is My Healer

Exodus 15:22–27

'I am the LORD, who heals you' (v. 26, NIV).

The children of Israel had been spared from death by the Passover lamb, freed from Pharaoh's oppressive rule, and led through the Red Sea. As they moved forward in freedom, they must have felt all their troubles were behind them.

But no sooner had they sung their song of gratitude and rejoicing than a new crisis appeared. Within three days, their song of deliverance had changed to a cry of despair. The water of the Red Sea had been too salty to drink, so they had pressed on to Marah in the hope of finding fresh water. They found to their horror that the water there was bitter and undrinkable.

Compared to the prospect of an agonising death from thirst, a sudden drowning in the water of the Red Sea must have looked appealing. They cried out to Moses and he cried out to the Lord, who guided Moses to a certain piece of wood, telling him to cast it into the water. Immediately the bitter water became sweet. The wood was not magical. The miracle of the incident was God's alone. What had been deadly was now life-giving, and the people drank, gained strength and went forward, confident that the Lord had delivered them again.

God used this powerful incident to speak a new name for himself – *Jehovah-Rophi* – the Lord is Healer. He promised that if the people would live in obedience to him, then he would not afflict them with any of the diseases that he brought upon the people of Egypt. He would always be with them as their healer. It was a simple but profound call – to trust and obey.

The wood that Moses was ordered to throw into the water is a parable of Calvary. Peter wrote, 'He himself bore our sins in his body on the tree, so that we might die to sins and live for righteousness; by his wounds you have been healed' (*1 Pet 2:24*).

To pray
Jehovah-Rophi, I ask you to bring healing to my deepest need today.

WEDNESDAY 16 MAY

Jehovah-Nissi – The Lord is My Banner

Exodus 17:8–16

'Moses built an altar and called it The LORD is my Banner'
(v. 15, NIV).

This graphic story is the only place in Scripture where the name *Jehovah-Nissi* is used, but the truth that his name is a banner of victory is often repeated.

In a place called Rephidim the Amalekites come to fight against Israel. These warring people were descendants of Amalek, a grandson of Esau. They were a fierce nomadic tribe who lived in the desert region of the Dead Sea. They made part of their livelihood by conducting frequent raids on other settlements and carrying off booty. They killed for pleasure. One of the greatest insults in Israelite culture was to call someone 'a friend of Amalek'. When the Israelites entered the region, the Amalekites saw this as a perfect opportunity for both pleasure and profit. But this hostile tribe was moving in on the wrong group – a people led by God!

Joshua, first mentioned in this narrative, is introduced simply by name. He is obviously the young assistant of Moses and his military commander. While Joshua goes down to the valley to fight, Moses, Aaron and Hur go up onto the hilltop to pray. With the staff of God, the symbol of the divine presence, in his hands, Moses encourages his men and prays for God's victory.

The fight, however, is long and severe, the fortunes of the battle swaying first to one side and then to the other. Moses observes that when he holds his hands up in prayer, Israel prevails. When, in sheer weariness, he lets them fall, Amalek gains the advantage.

To avoid defeat, his colleagues hold up his hands, until Amalek is conquered and Israel victorious. In celebration of this deliverance, Moses builds an altar and calls it *Jehovah-Nissi*. This is God's victory! Once again, he has provided miraculous resources for his people and given them victory. Once again his presence is proved, both to Israel and to Israel's enemies.

To reflect on
No matter how strong the enemy, or how continuous his attacks today, God is with us, arming us with strength, training our hands for battle (cf. Ps. 18:32,34).

THURSDAY 17 MAY
Jehovah-M'Kaddesh – The Lord Who Sanctifies

Exodus 31:12–18

'I am the LORD, who makes you holy' (v. 13, NIV).

My friend Mary was distressed. 'You know I told you that my new year's resolution was to be a better Christian?' she said. 'Well, ever since I said that, I've been grumpy and uptight. My husband and some of my non-Christian friends are saying, "Oh, you're just like the old Mary again!"' I knew exactly what Mary was battling. Her struggle is the same for most new believers. Even Paul knew something of this. 'The moment I decide to do good, sin is there to trip me up... I've tried everything and nothing helps. I'm at the end of my rope' (*Rom 7:21,24, The Message*).

When God chose a people to be a holy nation, he understood the struggle they would experience. In a world characterised by godlessness and sin, they were to be a people characterised by holiness. For the individual, that is hard enough. For a whole nation, that requirement seems impossible, were it not for *Jehovah-M'Kaddesh*, a name of God which speaks of his initiative in setting apart, and making holy, a people for himself.

God chose a people who would represent his way of life to the whole earth. This was at the heart of Abraham's calling. 'Abraham will surely become a great and powerful nation, and all nations on earth will be blessed through him. For I have chosen him... [I] will bring [it] about' (*Gen 18:18,19*). Through this nation, the Messiah would be born.

For a nation, as for an individual, the beginning point of holiness is always *Jehovah-M'Kaddesh*. Left to ourselves, the downward pull will always be too strong. But as God calls, so he enables. He commands, 'Sanctify yourselves', then speaks of the divine grace available. 'I am the LORD, who makes you holy' (*Lev 20:7,8*).

At the end of his rope, Paul found the answer – Jesus. My friend Mary is finding the same answer as she lives in close partnership with *Jehovah-M'Kaddesh* in the daily experience of her sanctification.

To reflect on
'You are a chosen people, a royal priesthood, a holy nation, a people belonging to God' (1 Pet 2:9).

FRIDAY 18 MAY

Adonai – Lord, Sovereign Master

Genesis 15:1–21

'Hear, O Israel: The LORD our God, the LORD is one'
(Deuteronomy 6:4, NIV).

The Old Testament command that 'anyone who blasphemes the name of the LORD must be put to death' (*Lev 24:16*) was so fearful for Jewish people that they would not say the holy name *Jehovah*. When scribes came to this name, they would often write the less awful name, *Adonai*, meaning 'my ruler' or 'Lord'.

Adonai first occurs in Genesis 15:2 where God, as Master Owner, was about to reveal to Abram how he would fulfil his promise to make him head of a great nation. The name implies authority, reverence and relationship. David said, 'My God (*Elohim*) and Lord (*Adonai*)' (*Ps 35:23*), the same words uttered by Thomas as he recognised the deity of the resurrected Jesus, 'My Lord and my God!' (*John 20:28*).

Used of God, the name *Adonai* is plural and possessive, meaning 'my Lords', confirming the idea of a trinity found in the name *Elohim*. So God is described as 'God of gods and Lord of lords' (*Deut 10:17*), which implies sovereignty above every other ruler.

Isaiah saw the Lord (*Adonai*) seated on a throne, 'high and exalted, and the train of his robe filled the temple' (*Isa 6:1*). He recognised him as the king, Lord of Hosts (*Jehovah-Tsebaoth*) and heard the voice of the Lord (*Adonai*) saying, 'Whom shall I send?' This vision and voice belonged to the sovereign God who called and commissioned him for service.

This name challenges us. Do I honour and love him as my *Adonai*? Does he have my allegiance, my commitment? Jesus himself pronounced judgment on those who call him 'Lord, Lord!' but do not recognise his lordship in their lives. Hudson Taylor often said, 'If he is not Lord of all, he is not Lord at all.'

God spoke to me with this name one day recently, as I fumed about a sudden change in my plans because someone had let me down. Gently he asked, 'Who's in charge round here?'

To reflect on

Who's in charge of you? 'You are not your own; you were bought at a price' (1 Cor 6:19,20).

SATURDAY 19 MAY
Jehovah-Shalom – The Lord is Peace

Judges 6:11–24

'Gideon built an altar to the LORD there and called it
The LORD is Peace' (v. 24, NIV).

The Midianites were a desert people descended from Abraham's second wife Keturah (*Gen 25:1,2*). From this relationship came a nation that was always in conflict with Israel. Years earlier the Israelites, while still wandering in the wilderness, fought the Midianites and almost destroyed them (*Num 31:1–20*). But because they failed to wipe them out completely, the tribe repopulated. Here they were once again oppressing Israel.

The nation of Israel by this time had turned away from God, and adopted many of the idols and religious practices of their heathen neighbours. The book of Judges tells of alternating periods of sin, slavery and sorrow, with the people in an endless, weary pattern of sinning and repenting.

The people were suffering at the hands of the Midianites, and God was suffering at their hardness of heart, when a messenger, the angel of the Lord, came to young Gideon. He was threshing wheat in a winepress, out of sight of any marauding Midianites. The angel's greeting, 'The Lord is with you, mighty warrior!' (*v. 12*), was met with a string of 'buts' from Gideon.

Gideon pleaded his unfitness for the task of fighting the enemy. He was not a military man, his clan had no reputation in warfare. But when God assured him that he would be with him and lead him to victory, he accepted the challenge. In commemoration, Gideon built an altar and named it *Jehovah-Shalom*, the Lord is Peace. That name was Gideon's greatest confidence for the future. The God who spoke peace to this terror-stricken servant would also bring peace to the nation.

How many Christians have stood, like Gideon, in a fearful place, trembling, inadequate, daunted by God's calling? 'Here am I, Lord, send someone else!' Yet God still delights to choose and use for his service those who consider themselves unequal to the task. To those who obey, *Jehovah-Shalom* gives his peace, transforming fear into faith.

To reflect on
'Peace I leave with you; my peace I give you ... do not be afraid' (*John 14:27*).

SUNDAY 20 MAY
In Trouble but Not Afraid

Psalm 3

'To the LORD I cry aloud, and he answers me from his holy hill'
(v. 4, NIV).

Psalm 3 is the first actual prayer in the book of Psalms, and is anchored in an historical moment when David is fleeing from his rebellious son Absalom and a host of traitors (2 Sam 15:14).

In two verses, David describes his desperate situation. His enemies are numerous, aggressive and mocking. His threefold anguish is matched by a threefold assurance. God covers his vulnerability as with a shield, the enemy taunts are eclipsed by the experience of God as his 'glory', and the overwhelming hostility which makes his head sink in discouragement is reversed by God raising his head in hope (v. 3). David's cry for help is answered.

At the centre of the psalm there is a picture of trust and confidence. 'I lie down, I go to sleep, I wake up again' (cf. v. 5). For David, these everyday actions are prayer, an expression of his trust in a God who protects and sustains him even while he sleeps. In spite of the multitudes arrayed against him, he is not afraid.

David then prays for victory, asking God to strike his enemies on the jaw and to break their teeth. These words are symbolic. To strike someone on the cheek or jaw was to insult them badly; to break someone's teeth was to render them speechless. Just as David has been hurt and insulted by the words of his enemies, so now he prays for them to be treated in the same way.

Such brutal words do not usually fit our picture of prayer. How can David utter such angry and vengeful prayers? Only by trust in a God to whom he could tell every thought and feeling and emotion, knowing that his honesty would be heard and understood. This prayer may not be 'nice', but it is certainly human!

The psalm ends on a note of confidence. Victory meant not only deliverance from an enemy, but also God's blessing upon his people.

Pray today for those for whom things are going wrong – that they won't blame God, but seek him!

MONDAY 21 MAY
Jehovah-Tsebaoth – The Lord of Hosts

Psalm 46

'The LORD of hosts is with us' (v. 7, AV).

'With a burst of brilliant wings and three trails of sparkling fire, the warriors shot into the sky, heading southward, becoming smaller and smaller until finally they were gone, leaving the now peaceful town of Ashton in very capable hands.' So ends Frank Peretti's novel *This Present Darkness*. Peretti's recent writings have done much to help Christians understand Paul's words, that 'our struggle is not against flesh and blood, but against the rulers, against the authorities and powers of this dark world and against the spiritual forces of evil in the heavenly realms' (*Eph 6:12*).

In this cosmic battle in which we are all engaged, the name *Jehovah-Tsebaoth* speaks victory, for he is the Lord God of Hosts. This name is used many times in Scripture to describe the vast power and rule of God.

He is Lord of the stellar hosts. 'Thus the heavens and the earth were completed in all their vast array' (*Gen 2:1*).

He is Lord of all animal hosts. He has promised that one day 'the wolf will live with the lamb, the leopard will lie down with the goat ... and a little child will lead them' (*Isa 11:6*).

He is Lord of all angelic hosts. No matter how great the odds against God's people, there are invisible and invincible divine forces engaged on our behalf. 'The chariots of God are tens of thousands and thousands of thousands' (*Ps 68:17*).

He is Lord of all human hosts. Powerful men like Napoleon and Hitler may strut across the world's stage, but *Jehovah-Tsebaoth* is the supreme Lord of history.

He is Lord of the satanic hosts. At Calvary, Satan was defeated. When Jesus cried out, 'It is finished', he was declaring victory over the unseen rulers of the darkness.

The title *Jehovah-Tsebaoth* embraces both the heavenly and the earthly reign of God. This great Lord of Hosts who rules the world is also guardian and helper of all who put their trust in him.

Lord, God of hosts, be with us yet;
Lest we forget – lest we forget!
    ('Recessional' by Rudyard Kipling)

TUESDAY 22 MAY

Jehovah-Rohi – The Lord is My Shepherd

Psalm 23

'The LORD is my shepherd, I shall not be in want' (v. 1, NIV).

The children of Israel were a pilgrim people, always on the move, always in need of divine protection and provision. The name of God as *Jehovah-Rohi* was a revelation of One whose shepherd love, care and resources they could depend upon in all the unknown twists and turns of their wilderness journey. No matter how helpless and needy they felt, their faithful shepherd would be present to guard and guide them.

The metaphor of the shepherd is found in Scripture as early as Jacob's blessing to Joseph before he died. The aged patriarch gave testimony to the unfailing goodness of God, speaking of 'the God who has been my shepherd all my life to this day' (*Gen 48:15*).

A later shepherd, David, used the same image in his famous 'Shepherd' psalm. From the days of watching sheep out on the hillside near Bethlehem and protecting them against bears and lions, David had become shepherd-king to the people of Israel, providing for and protecting them. In the same way, the Lord was with him as a shepherd. David's sevenfold testimony in Psalm 23 – 'he makes, he leads, he restores, he guides, you are with me, you prepare, you anoint' – speaks of the completeness of the care of God for his people.

Moses named God as *Jehovah* – holy, awesome and unapproachable. David named him as *Jehovah-Rohi* – the tender, caring shepherd who tends his flock, gathers them in his arms and carries them close to his heart (see *Isa 40:11*). This powerful Old Testament picture is further illuminated by Jesus who came as the Good Shepherd to seek and save the lost. When he rose from the dead, he was named the Great Shepherd (*Heb 13:20*) and will one day return as the Chief Shepherd (*1 Pet 5:4*).

Today, God calls his people into partnership with him in the task of shepherding. We hear echoes of Jesus' call to Peter, 'Feed my lambs... take care of my sheep... feed my sheep' (*John 21:15–17*).

To sing today
'Shepherd of my soul, I give you full control,
Wherever you may lead, I will follow...'

WEDNESDAY 23 MAY
El Shaddai – The Breasted God

Psalm 91

'He who dwells in the shelter of the Most High will rest in the shadow of the Almighty' (v. 1, NIV).

I was a long way from home. The sunny African morning was eclipsed by an overwhelming darkness within me. Needing specialist hospital treatment, I had been driven to Lusaka and left on my own to wait for the afternoon appointment. I felt abandoned and afraid of what lay ahead. Was this to be the end of the dream of missionary service that my husband and I had long prepared for?

As I cried out to God, he led me to Psalm 91. Reading the first verses, I was given a picture of a mother hen stretching her wing over her chicks in protection. In that moment, the darkness of abandonment became the comforting shadow of God's arm, stretched out in protection, gathering me to himself, holding me safe.

El Shaddai, usually translated 'God Almighty', has a powerful metaphor behind it that now, twenty-four years on as I write this, makes that mother hen image even more significant. Scholars say that the word *Shaddai* is derived from the word used in Scripture for a woman's breast. Some scholars have been bold enough to use this name to speak of 'the mother-love of God'. The idea of almightiness is fully expressed in the word *El*. The word *Shaddai* goes further, and suggests perfect supply, protection and comfort. As a name for God, it literally means 'the almighty breasted one'.

This name for God is first used in Genesis 17:1 where God speaks his loving reassurance and compassion to Abraham, weary from long years of testing, and the long-deferred hopes of ever having a son.

The same name is spoken thirty-one times to suffering Job, reminding him in the midst of his trials of the mighty, tender love of God.

The same name was spoken to me on that Zambian morning, transforming my inner darkness into the reassurance of God's protection and love.

To reflect on
'To gather sustenance and consolation from the bosom of God is to be made strong for all the pilgrimage.'
(Dr G. Campbell Morgan)

THURSDAY 24 MAY
Jehovah-Hoseenu – The Lord Our Maker

Psalm 95

'Come, let us bow down in worship, let us kneel before the
LORD our Maker' (v. 6, NIV).

Psalm 95 is an expression of joyful celebration of God as King and Shepherd. The great God, who is King over all the gods, is hailed as the Creator of the earth and the sea. As members of his flock, we are invited to approach him in worship.

The Hebrew word *asah* as applied to God as our Maker does not refer to his work in creation, when he caused things to come into being, but to his ability to fashion something out of what already exists. It has the idea of forming, shaping, moulding. Abraham looked forward to 'a city with foundations, whose architect and builder is God' (*Heb 11:10*). As *Jehovah-Hoseenu*, God is building his people together into a dwelling in which he lives by his Spirit (see *Eph 2:22*).

Paul reminds us that we are his 'workmanship' (*Eph 2:10*), his 'work of art'. Literally, 'we are God's poem'.

The film *Mr Holland's Opus* tells the story of a man who spent thirty years teaching music to high-school students. He poured himself out for his students. The great passion and longing of his life was to write a symphony, but there was never enough time. The day came when he was no longer needed at the school. As he was leaving, he walked into the assembly hall and found a crowd of students, some from thirty years back. They had come to thank him.

The spokeswoman, a former student and now a well-known public figure, said, 'Mr Holland, you may feel your life has been wasted. You didn't ever get your symphony written. You have never become rich or famous. But look around. Each one of us in this room is a better person because of you. We, your pupils, are your symphony. We are the melodies and notes of your great work, the music of your life.'

To reflect on
That is how God looks at you. Sing to him today:
'Spirit of the living God, fall afresh on me.
Break me, melt me, mould me, fill me.'

FRIDAY 25 MAY

Jehovah-Tsidkenu – The Lord is Our Righteousness

Jeremiah 23:1–8

'This is the name by which he will be called:
The LORD Our Righteousness' (v. 6, NIV).

The prophet Jeremiah expressed the anguished heart-cry of God concerning those whom he had called to be leaders of his people. Instead of shepherding the flock in their care, they were scattering them. The whole kingdom of Judah was hastening to its fall; its leaders corrupt, neglectful, irresponsible.

But while flashing forth his word of condemnation, Jeremiah also spoke a word of hope. In spite of the coming judgment against his people, God would be faithful to his covenant and the promises he had made. Jehovah God would raise up a Righteous Branch, a perfect king who would sprout from the roots of David's fallen dynasty to reign over the whole earth, bringing peace and security to Israel. His name would be *Jehovah-Tsidkenu* – the Lord is our Righteousness. This name of God is a great Messianic title.

The theme of righteousness sweeps through the whole of Scripture. The Greeks sought wisdom. The Romans wanted power and world dominion. The nation of Israel sought after God and the keeping of his laws. In their passionate desire for righteousness they discovered their unrighteousness, and how far short of the divine standard they fell. So they became the people of the penitential psalm, seekers after purity, longing for communion with a holy God. Goodness and integrity were of far greater value than wealth and the ways of the world. *Jehovah-Tsidkenu*, the Lord is our Righteousness, was the one they followed.

For those ancient seekers after righteousness, and for us today, the promise is that, as we hunger and thirst for righteousness, we will be filled (*Matt 5:6*). In Jesus our righteousness is made possible, for he has died for our sins, and lives his righteous life in us. Jesus is now our *Jehovah-Tsidkenu*.

To reflect on
Christ Jesus 'has become for us wisdom from God – that is, our righteousness, holiness and redemption' (1 Cor 1:30). May this great truth make you walk tall today.

SATURDAY 26 MAY

Jehovah-Shammah – The Lord is There

Ezekiel 48:30–35

'And the name of the city from that time on will be:
THE LORD IS THERE' (v. 35, NIV).

This title is the last of the divine names in the Old Testament. The names given to God have expressed the unfolding of his purposes for all mankind. He is the Lord who provides a ransom for sinners, who heals our diseases, who is our banner in conflict, our sanctifier, our peace-giver, our shepherd, our righteousness.

Now, as a climax to the revelation of God, this decisive name promises God's permanent presence with his people. It is a name that people right through the Scriptures, and beyond, have proven to be true.

Jacob, forced to flee because of his own trickery, slept in a desolate place with his head on a stone pillow and had a vision of angels. Waking in astonishment, he declared, 'Surely Jehovah is in this place and I didn't know it.'

The psalmist wondered where he could go to get away from God's presence, and found there was nowhere. Jonah experienced the same in a very unlikely place – the belly of a great fish.

The woman who came to the well at an unusual time of day to avoid other women, met instead *Jehovah-Shammah* in the person of Jesus, who set her free from her past and gave her living water to drink.

Brother Lawrence practised God's presence in the midst of his pots and pans in the monastery kitchen. David Livingstone took to Africa the promise of Jesus, 'Lo, I am with you always, to the very end of the world!' Livingstone would add, 'That's the word of a perfect gentleman, and that's the end of it!'

Mary Slessor, the 'uncrowned Queen of Calabar' once said, 'If I have ever done anything it is because he always went in front.' John Bunyan, in Bedford prison for his faithful witness, confessed that his Saviour came into his cell and that every stone shone like jasper.

And so the stories could go on as I tell my story and you tell yours. From eternity past, to eternity in the future, God is called *Jehovah-Shammah*.

To reflect on
There can be no doubt about his presence with you today!

PENTECOST MEDITATIONS
Introduction

In the Jewish calendar, the Day of Pentecost was a regular, recurring, expected occasion. Pentecost was the name of the Jewish festival held fifty days after the Sabbath that followed Passover – the word Pentecost simply meaning 'fiftieth'. It was a festival that celebrated the first-fruits of the harvest and the giving of the Law to Moses on Mount Sinai.

But on the Day of Pentecost following the resurrection of our Lord something happened that was unexpected, unorganised, vivid, exciting. We see a group of Christ's disciples huddled in an upper room in Jerusalem as instructed, awaiting the fulfilment of their Master's promise: 'Do not leave Jerusalem, but wait for the gift my Father promised, which you have heard me speak about... in a few days you will be baptised with the Holy Spirit' (*Acts 1:4-5*).

The disciples were in an intensity of prayer the like of which they had never known before. They prayed for ten days, and on the tenth day, the fiftieth day after the miracle of the resurrection, a new miracle occurred.

When the disciples later tried to explain what had happened, they spoke of a sound like the blowing of a violent wind coming from heaven and filling the house. They talked of seeing what seemed to be tongues of fire that separated and came to rest on each of them. They recalled being enabled by the Spirit to speak in strange languages. But each of those attempts at an explanation was but a sign, an inadequate symbol pointing to an experience that was essentially inexplicable. It was a life-changing experience for them and for the world!

In the Pentecost meditations of the next fifteen days, Colonel Earl Robinson focuses on some of the implications of that life-changing experience for the disciples of the first century of the Christian Church and for disciples of today.

Colonel Robinson is a Salvation Army officer who has been in pastoral, administrative and teaching appointments in Canada, including that of the founding President of the William and Catherine Booth College. He is currently in an International Headquarters appointment. He and his wife Benita are the Secretary and Associate Secretary for Spiritual Life Development and International External Relations. They also serve as the Chair and Secretary of the International Doctrine Council. Their point of operation is in the Greater Vancouver area of British Columbia, Canada.

SUNDAY 27 MAY
The Spirit's Filling

Acts 2:1–4

'All of them were filled with the Holy Spirit' (v. 4a, NIV).

The essentially inexplicable Pentecost experience that Christ's disciples could only describe in strange symbols was this: they had been 'filled' with the Holy Spirit.

They knew about the Holy Spirit before the day of Pentecost. They knew what their Lord had said to Nicodemus about being born again of the Holy Spirit, starting a new kind of life through the living, indwelling Spirit of God (John 3:5–8). They realised that they, too, had started a new kind of life, enabling their Lord to say that they could rejoice because their names were written in heaven (Luke 10:20). They understood what the apostle Paul was later to teach – that 'if anyone does not have the Spirit of Christ, he does not belong to Christ' (Rom 8:9); that all true followers of Jesus 'have' the Holy Spirit, are indwelt by him, have the gift of his presence, the beginning gift of life in the Spirit.

However, something new happened for those disciples on that Day of Pentecost following their Lord's resurrection. They were not only indwelt by the Spirit, but 'filled' with the Spirit. It was not just a beginning of life in the Spirit, there was now a fullness to that life.

The disciples faced an about-turn in their lives when they first met Jesus and decided to follow him as Lord and Master. They became new creatures in Christ. But on the Day of Pentecost there was another about-turn. Something so dramatic happened, because of their being filled with the Holy Spirit, that they were never the same again in what they were able to be and to do for their Lord. Many wonders and miraculous signs were done through them (Acts 2:43). They lived together in harmony (Acts 2:44). They were able to speak the word of God boldly (Acts 4:31). Multitudes believed in the Lord because of their influence (Acts 5:14). They were a changed people from the little group huddled in the upper room in Jerusalem before the Day of Pentecost.

To ponder
Because of Pentecost, the disciples were filled with confidence because they had been filled with the Spirit!

MONDAY 28 MAY
The Spirit's Filling Today

Ephesians 5:15–20

'Be filled with the Spirit' (v. 18b, NIV).

The Day of Pentecost which followed the resurrection of our Lord was a unique day that ushered in the age of the Spirit and established the birth of the Church. But the experience that came upon those gathered together for that day was not intended to be a unique once-for-all experience never to be repeated with any other company of believers.

On the contrary, it was to become the norm. That is the Pentecostal significance of the prophecy quoted by Peter from Joel: 'I will pour out my Spirit on *all* people' (*Acts 2:17*). The Spirit's filling is not just for the spiritually elite, for a minority of the people of God, as seemed to be the case in the Old Testament era. It is not just for prophet, priest and king.

When under the inspiration of the Spirit the apostle Paul later enjoins the Ephesian Christians to be 'filled with the Spirit' (*Eph 5:18*), he is uttering a divine injunction for the followers of Christ in every age. In essence he is saying the following:

- Be not only born again of the Spirit and indwelt by the Spirit, but be controlled and cleansed and filled by the Spirit.
- Don't be content with a weak and defective commitment to your Lord and an accompanying partial awareness of the presence of the Spirit of God.
- Let your commitment to the Lord be complete so that God has all there is of you.
- Allow God to direct your mind and emotions and will and body and soul and spirit, so that you become a whole and healthy and effective servant of his by his Holy Spirit filling you to overflowing.

Prayer
To make our weak hearts strong and brave,
  Send the fire!
To live a dying world to save,
  Send the fire!
O see us on thy altar lay
Our lives, our all, this very day,
To crown the offering now we pray,
  Send the fire!
            (William Booth, SASB 203)

TUESDAY 29 MAY
The Spirit's Power

Zechariah 4:6–10

' "Not by might nor by power, but by my Spirit," says the LORD Almighty' (v. 6, NIV).

I wonder if that word of the Lord through the prophet Zechariah to Zerubbabel would have been recalled by the disciples of our Lord following their Pentecost experience.

Zerubbabel was the leader of the Jewish people at the time of the return of the Israelites from their captivity in Babylon. On arriving in Jerusalem his great work was to be the rebuilding of the temple, and he set about that task immediately. The foundation of the temple was laid quickly, but there followed a long suspension of sixteen years when no temple construction seemed to be done. The Israelites were building costly houses for themselves, but they were neglecting God's house.

Then the spirit of prophecy blazed up among the returned captives. The initial inspiration was given through the prophet Haggai, renewed and reinforced by Zechariah as he foresaw that God's temple could be completed, but not through the political strength or the building enterprises of Zerubbabel alone or any other human leader.

So it is that Zechariah brings the word of the Lord to Zerubbabel indicating that, if he would trust the Spirit of God, the great mountain of difficulty that confronted him could become level ground. He could complete the temple that had been begun. And the final placing of the headstone would be greeted with shouts of joy and thanksgiving. Even those who had despised the unpromising small beginnings in the temple's building would rejoice as they saw the construction brought to completion at the hands of Zerubbabel – through the Spirit.

Whether or not the disciples of our Lord would have recalled that incident on the Day of Pentecost, their experience was to be similar. They were to find, as the apostle Paul put it, that 'the weakness of God is stronger than man's strength' (*1 Cor 1:25*). Their strength to do the Lord's work was to come from the Spirit's power!

To ponder
Success in God's work depends not upon human might or power, but on the divine Spirit.

WEDNESDAY 30 MAY
The Spirit's Power Today

Ephesians 3:13–21

'I pray that out of his glorious riches he may strengthen you with power through his Spirit in your inner being' (v. 16, NIV).

By what means are we to build temples today? By might? power? hard work? the strength of hand and mind and talent? the power of activity and service?

It is true that God has chosen humanity through whom to do his work in his world and that he relies on us to do what he has called us to do. Yet it is also true that the might of activity and the strength of hard work in themselves accomplish little for God and his kingdom, that organisation simply for the sake of organisation can be an encumbrance in the service of Christ, that 'busyness' can fool a person into spiritual complacency.

We need constantly to be reminded that it is not by our might that things are accomplished for the Lord, but only by his might working through us. Paul implies that in Ephesians 3:16 when he prays for the Ephesian Christians that God would grant them, out of his glorious riches, to be strengthened with power through his Spirit in their inner being.

It is not by our power that true temples are built and men and women and boys and girls fill those temples to God's glory. That happens only when we rely on the promise of his power: 'But you will receive power when the Holy Spirit comes on you; and you will be my witnesses in Jerusalem, and in all Judea and Samaria, and to the ends of the earth' (*Acts 1:8*). That is but one reference in the book of Acts to the importance of the power of the Spirit in the Church and in its members. There are some fifty-nine such references, causing some commentators to refer to the book of Acts as the 'Acts of the Holy Spirit'.

The power of the Spirit is our enablement for Christian ministry and for Christian living. And what an enablement that is! Through the fullness of God's Spirit in our inner being, we are strengthened by 'him who is able to do immeasurably more than all we ask or imagine, according to his power that is at work within us' (*Eph 3:20*).

Prayer
Spirit of the living God,
Fall afresh on me.
Break me, melt me, mould me, fill me;
Spirit of the living God,
Fall afresh on me.
          (SASB, chorus section, 53)

THURSDAY 31 MAY
The Spirit's Purity

Acts 15:1–11

'He made no distinction between us and them, for he purified their hearts by faith' (v. 9, NIV).

As noted in our first Pentecost meditation (*WoL 27 May 2000*), in Acts 2 we have the account of the disciples in Jerusalem being filled with the Holy Spirit on the Day of Pentecost which followed the resurrection: 'All of them were filled with the Holy Spirit' (*Acts 2:4*).

Later, in Acts 10, we have the account of the Holy Spirit coming upon the Gentiles at Caesarea in a similar fashion. Peter was visiting there after a vision had revealed to him that God had no favourites between Jews and Gentiles. He was preaching to them concerning the Christ, and in Acts 10:44–45 we read this: 'While Peter was still speaking these words, the Holy Spirit came on all who heard the message. The circumcised believers who had come with Peter were astonished that the gift of the Holy Spirit had been poured out even on the Gentiles.'

In Acts 15, Peter links together the disciples' filling of Acts 2 and the Gentiles' experience in the Spirit in Acts 10, emphasising what was apparently the most pronounced impression of what had happened in both instances: 'He made no distinction between us and them, for he purified their hearts by faith' (*Acts 15:9*). What he was saying was that 'just as our hearts were purified when we were filled with the Spirit, so their hearts were also purified through their experience in the Spirit'.

When the disciples in Jerusalem knew the experience of being filled with the Spirit, they testified to seeing 'what seemed to be tongues of fire that separated and came to rest on each of them' (*Acts 2:3*). The reference to 'fire' may be a reference to the cleansing fire of the Holy Spirit. It was fire like that of the fiery coal from the altar that cleansed the lips of Isaiah at the time of his vision of the Holy God, and the accompanying recognition of his own uncleanness (*Isa 6:6–7*).

To ponder
The heart cannot be filled with the Holy Spirit until that heart has been emptied of self-centredness and selfishness and sin – refined of that which is impure.

FRIDAY 1 JUNE
The Spirit's Purity Today

Galatians 5:16–21

'So I say, live by the Spirit, and you will not gratify the desires of the sinful nature' (v. 16, NIV).

Our part in ensuring that we are refined of that which is impure is to live by the Spirit and allow the Spirit's purity to live in us.

We have an awareness of the purifying influence of the Holy Spirit when we are born again of the Spirit, when we realise that Jesus died that we might be forgiven, he died to make us good (*SASB 133*). But the power of sin may still overcome us so that we do not do what we really want to do and seem rather to be controlled by our sinful nature (*Gal 5:17*). Paul speaks about that in his letter to the Romans as well when he says, 'Now if I do what I do not want to do, it is no longer I who do it, but it is sin living in me that does it' (*Rom 7:20*).

'Sin living in me' – there's a sense of despair in that recognition. It's the feeling that apparently there's been only a surface change – sins forgiven, the outward life different, but inside still the same person with selfish motives, ego-building designs, impure thoughts, the power of sin still dominant.

That power of sin needs to be dealt with by a cleansing that goes beyond the surface to the depths of our personality. As on the Day of Pentecost for the disciples, our 'hearts' need to be purified.

The biblical concept of the heart relates to the centre of one's personality so that such a purifying is a cleansing in depth, a purity which interpenetrates to every part of one's being, which deals not only with surface sins, but with the sin principle, the sin power. And that has to do with the Spirit's purity in us.

A reliance on the Spirit's purity means living by the Spirit and allowing the cleansing fire of the Holy Spirit to invade our being completely and in depth, so that we are no longer predominantly controlled by the weaknesses and frailty of unaided human nature but have been redirected by him.

Prayer
Burning, burning, deeply burning,
  Deeply burning holy Fire,
Now, your perfect plan discerning,
  Your design is my desire.
            (John Gowans, SASB 206)

SATURDAY 2 JUNE
The Spirit's Gifts

Romans 12:3–8

'We have different gifts, according to the grace given us' (v. 6, NIV).

The teaching of Scripture is that every Christian has at least one of the Spirit's gifts, one service gift bestowed on him or her by the Holy Spirit.

There are five primary passages in Scripture on spiritual gifts. Each presents the teaching in a slightly different fashion. Besides Romans 12:6 quoted above, key verses in the other four passages are as follows:

- from *1 Corinthians 12:4–11*: 'Now to each one the manifestation of the Spirit is given for the common good' (v. 7);
- from *1 Corinthians 12:27–31*: 'But eagerly desire the greater gifts' (v. 31);
- from *Ephesians 4:4–13*: 'But to each one of us grace has been given as Christ apportioned it' (v. 7);
- from *1 Peter 4:7–11*: 'Each one should use whatever gift he has received to serve others, faithfully administering God's grace in its various forms' (v. 10).

There is a similarity between spiritual gifts and natural talents. For example, both natural talents and spiritual gifts must be discovered and cultivated. Both can be allowed to fall into disuse. But the major difference is this – while natural talents may be developed and used solely for personal satisfaction, gifts of the Spirit are related to the body life of the Church. They are endowments through which the Holy Spirit channels his life-giving power. Through his gifting, the disciples of Christ convey his life to the life of the Christian community and of the world.

That does not mean that one's spiritual gifts cannot be a source of deep personal satisfaction. Although those gifts are primarily outgoing in relation to the Church's body life, a proper stewardship of spiritual gifts has a reflex effect upon the individual. Christians use their gifts as a blessing for others, but they are blessed by that use as well.

To ponder
To cooperate with the Holy Spirit in developing and using the gifts that he provides brings fulfilment to the individual disciple of Christ as well as blessings to the Church and to the world.

SUNDAY 3 JUNE
The Spirit's Gifts Today

Ephesians 4:4–13

'It was he who gave some to be apostles, some to be prophets, some to be evangelists, and some to be pastors and teachers, to prepare God's people for works of service, so that the body of Christ may be built up' (vv. 11,12, NIV).

Many of the gifts of the Spirit describe activities expected of every Christian to some degree – as for example the gifts of serving, encouraging, giving and mercy (Rom 12:7–8). Besides being spiritual gifts provided in greater measure to some, these are roles of ministry that ought to be exemplified in the lives of all Christians.

Then, too, there are some responsibilities that come to certain people by virtue of positions that they hold in the Church. One does not necessarily need a sense of spiritual giftedness to carry out the functions of such positions responsibly.

In our reading for today there are five spiritual gifts that are related to the role of leadership within the Church of Christ – the gifts of being apostle (a leader with a strong sense of mission), prophet (a leader who communicates the word of God with clarity), evangelist (a leader who brings people to commitment to Christ), pastor (a leader with a caring spirit for others) and teacher (a leader who grounds others in God's truth). Few if any Christian leaders have all five of those gifts.

What today's text suggests, however, is that the leader's primary responsibility is this – to help others to discover and develop and use their spiritual gifts for the building up of the body of Christ. Leaders are called to encourage members of the body to believe that they are gifted, to understand what their gifts are, to develop those gifts, and to accept responsibilities through which their gifts might be used. If leaders are faithful to this call, and if all parts of the body use their gifts for the glory of God, the body of Christ will be built up.

We all have our individual parts to play in today's Church – in doing what needs to be done, and in seeking to discover and do what we do best!

Prayer
O use me, Lord, use even me,
Just as thou wilt and when and where.
    (Frances Ridley Havergal, SASB 612)

MONDAY 4 JUNE
The Spirit's Fruit

Galatians 5:22–26

'But the fruit of the Spirit is love' (v. 22, NIV).

A reference to the fruit of the Holy Spirit accompanies every one of the primary passages on the gifts of the Spirit in Scripture (see *Rom 12:9-10, Eph 5:2, 1 Pet 4:8*, and *1 Cor 13* which goes with the two passages in *1 Cor 12*). The suggestion is that the fruit of the Spirit is a prerequisite for an effective exercise of the gifts of the Spirit.

Love stands at the head of the listing of the fruit of the Spirit in Galatians 5:22–23. The singular use of 'fruit' may be used instead of the plural because of there being one essential fruit of the Spirit from which the other eight graces are derived. That fruit is love, an unconquerable love that loves no matter what!

It is in Christ that we see what love really is, love that caused him to leave his place in glory to stoop to us at our points of need; that moved him to reach out his hand and touch a leper; that wept over a city that would not repent; that sorrowed over disciples who were jealous of one another; that loved those who could only sleep while he prayed, as on the eve of the crucifixion; that led him to die on the cross for a world that seemed to many to be unlovable.

When, by the grace of the Holy Spirit, we approach a love like that in our own lives, such love leads to the other fruits of the Spirit. It leads to joy whose basis is in God himself; to a peace that passes earthly understanding; to patience even with those who may treat us unjustly; to a kindness that tries to understand the situations of others before judging them; to goodness that is 'love with her sleeves rolled up' (Frederick Coutts); to faithfulness that is reliable in relationships; to gentleness that is considerate; to self-control that enables us to be a servant to others because we are not enslaved by our own uncontrollable selfishness.

To ponder
'Love is patient, love is kind. It does not envy, it does not boast, it is not proud. It is not rude, it is not self-seeking, it is not easily angered, it keeps no record of wrongs. Love does not delight in evil but rejoices with the truth. It always protects, always trusts, always hopes, always perseveres. Love never fails.'
(1 Cor 13:4–8)

TUESDAY 5 JUNE
The Spirit's Fruit Today

1 Corinthians 13:1–13

'And now these three remain: faith, hope and love. But the greatest of these is love' (v. 13, NIV).

The world has always needed love, and it yearns for that fruit of the Spirit today. As disciples of our Lord, we can contribute nothing more valuable to this world than love, so that the opening three verses of 1 Corinthians 13 are as true today as they were when first uttered.

To speak in the tongues of men, having the gift of being able to communicate clearly – that is a gift so needed in Christian witness today. To have the tongues of angels, perhaps having to do with an inexpressible heart language to God – that too is recognised as one of the gifts of the Spirit. But either form of verbal expression is not nearly so important as inward motivation, the quality of love. By themselves they are of little more value than the resounding gong or clanging symbol of pagan worship in the first century AD.

The gift of prophecy – being able to speak the word of God concerning contemporary and future issues, proclaiming God's word, written so that it reveals the Word made flesh in Christ – that is a gift to be desired. To understand all mysteries, having the gift of wisdom to discern spiritual things and understand the mind of God – that too is a gift of the Spirit that the world needs to see in disciples of Christ today. To have knowledge of truth, the power of comprehension – that is a particular gift of the Spirit required in this age of intellect. Each of those gifts is valuable in the economy of God. But Paul says that if we have those gifts without love, we have nothing.

It is good to have the gift of faith that can move mountains, that believes for miracles, that sets goals that can be achieved by a reliance on the power of God. But faith without love might desire to move mountains only to throw them into the path of someone else, so that without love, it is nothing.

Giving all we possess to the poor and even becoming martyrs for our faith if necessary – those are areas of action and service that can be of value to the kingdom of God. But if service is not motivated by love, it is of little value.

The fruit of the Spirit that is a love like that of Christ – that fruit is above all!

Prayer
His Spirit helping me,
Like him I'll be.

(John Gowans,
SASB chorus section, 107)

WEDNESDAY 6 JUNE
The Spirit's Guidance

Acts 13:1–3

'The Holy Spirit said, "Set apart for me Barnabas and Saul for the work to which I have called them" ' (v. 2, NIV).

In the book of Acts there is abounding evidence that when the disciples of the early Church became aware of the fullness of the Holy Spirit, they became acutely sensitive to his leadings.

When Philip was on his journey from Samaria to Gaza it was the Spirit who told him to approach the chariot of the man from Ethiopia. His obedience to that prompting allowed him to interpret the Old Testament Scriptures in the light of the person of Christ and lead a man to salvation (Acts 8:26–39).

When Peter had doubts as to whether he ought to mingle with the ceremonially unclean Gentile community, the Spirit told him to go to Caesarea. Because of his obedience to that message, Peter was used of God to reveal that the message of the gospel is for all peoples, not just the Israelites (Acts 10–11).

And in our Scripture reading today, when there was a need for missionaries to take the gospel of Christ throughout the then-known world, it was the Spirit who provided guidance for the first missionary journey of the apostle Paul. The Spirit had first of all called Barnabas and Saul (Paul) to that work, and then led the church in Antioch to set them apart and send them off for the fulfilment of their mission.

The Spirit's guidance was available to the church at Antioch and to the early disciples through his word written in the Scriptures of the Old Testament and through the teaching of Christ handed down to them. But there were special details of guidance which were not clearly known to them from the written word: the particular way in which the Lord's great commission of evangelisation was to be fulfilled, and those who were to be the leaders for that mission in the first century of the Church.

How were those details made known? The Holy Spirit spoke to the church at Antioch and called Barnabas and Saul to missionary leadership. And equally important – the church and its disciples responded positively to the Spirit's guidance.

To ponder
Was the Spirit's special guidance a peculiarity of the apostolic age, or does the Holy Spirit so guide the followers of Christ still?

THURSDAY 7 JUNE
The Spirit's Guidance Today

Acts 20:17–24

'And now, compelled by the Spirit, I am going to Jerusalem, not knowing what will happen to me there' (v. 22, NIV).

We can only conjecture as to whether or not the voice of the Holy Spirit's guidance was heard audibly by the first-century disciples of the Christian Church. We are aware that normally that is not his means of providing guidance today.

As with them, the Spirit's guidance is available to us through his word written in the Old Testament. And for us there is an increased measure of general guidance available to us in the Holy-Spirit-inspired New Testament. Nevertheless, there are still special details of guidance for which we today need to hear a direct word from the Spirit.

The testimony of God's people is that God the Holy Spirit does provide guidance today. He may guide through a variety of means: a book, a song, the influence and life of another, an inward Holy-Spirit-inspired intuition, an awareness that the circumstances of life are leading in one direction and that is God's direction, the fellowship of believers, God-directed reason, the intimacy of prayer communion with the Lord. Catherine Marshall said of the experience of her husband in *A Man Called Peter* that 'if a man or woman really wants to know the will of God, somehow God gets through to that person'.

The human problem is not so much in knowing God's will as it is in doing the will of God. Often we don't really want to know the Spirit's leadings, or we are not willing to be obedient to his guidance, because that might disturb our complacency. We want to follow an easier path, a path of our own making, instead of being obedient to the Spirit.

That surely must also have been the experience of the apostle Paul in the circumstances recounted in today's reading. It was the Spirit through whom he felt compelled to return to Jerusalem. He feared that prison and hardships would face him as a result, but he went because the Spirit told him to go. And because of that obedience he was able to complete the task given to him by the Lord, to testify to the gospel of God's grace even in the imprisonment of Rome.

Prayer
'Here am I. Send me!' (Isa 6:8b).

FRIDAY 8 JUNE
The Spirit's Comfort

John 14:1–17

'And I will pray the Father, and he shall give you another Comforter, that he may abide with you for ever; Even the Spirit of truth'
(vv. 16–17a, AV).

It was the night before the crucifixion and Jesus was with his disciples in the Upper Room. We can picture him looking around and realising what a weak lot those disciples really were, so dependent on his own guidance and encouragement. He had told them that he would now be with them just a little longer (*John 13:33*). What would they do without him? He could sense that it seemed to them as though their world was about to cave in. Their hearts were troubled.

To whom could they go for strength and guidance once Christ was gone? Could they find strength in the leadership of Peter who would so soon show weakness himself in denying the Lord whom he had said he would never fail? Could they rely on someone like John who had been so self-centred and so quick to lose his temper?

But just as their fears seemed to cause them to collapse under the thought of their loss, Jesus said, 'Let not your heart be troubled: ye believe in God, believe also in me... And I will pray the Father, and he shall give you another Comforter, that he may abide with you for ever; Even the Spirit of truth' (*John 14:1, 16–17, AV*).

The word translated as 'Comforter' in the Authorised Version speaks of the Holy Spirit coming as one 'with strength', 'with bravery'. His presence enables the dispirited person to be brave, to cope with things, to deal with inadequacies, to face any event of life or death, to know strength during the continuing battles of temptation and sin and disappointment. And the Holy Spirit became all of that to the disciples of our Lord in their future days.

The term is translated in other versions as 'Advocate' (*NRSV*) or 'Counsellor' (*NIV*). In that sense the Holy Spirit became for the disciples the one called alongside to help, the one ever available to provide counsel for every situation of life. They were not going to be alone after all!

To ponder
We all come to days of trouble and loneliness. On such days, an awareness that we are not alone because of the Spirit's presence can provide comfort and dispel loneliness.

SATURDAY 9 JUNE
The Spirit's Comfort Today

John 14:18–31

'I will not leave you comfortless: I will come to you' (v. 18, AV).

In our text of yesterday, Jesus told the disciples that the Father would give them 'another' Comforter. The term 'another' implies one like himself, one who would encourage, guide and strengthen as he had done. And in our text of today he so identifies himself with the coming of the Holy Spirit that it is almost as if he is talking about his other self.

The relationship between God the Son and God the Holy Spirit is part of the mystery of the Trinity. Taken together, our texts of yesterday and today particularly point to the Holy Spirit not being unreal or unknown when he would come with comfort to the disciples – he was to be like Christ. That is a special message concerning the Spirit's comforting presence for us today.

The Holy Spirit is the same God revealed in the Christ who understands the human situation and knows our needs. The doctrine of the Holy Spirit teaches that the one who ascended, the one who is 'up there', is also the one who is 'down here' in the person of his Holy Spirit. That means that the ever-living, ever-loving Christ is also, through his Spirit, ever-present for us.

A loved one is lost, and friends extend sympathy, but their presence brings little relief from an aching and lonely heart. We have tried to do that which is good, but have been misunderstood, not appreciated, and we feel that no one cares. We love and there is no love in return. There is physical or mental anguish that we suffer alone. But then the Holy Spirit comes alongside to help as a comforter and counsellor. And he strengthens our troubled hearts with the same ministry known by the early disciples when they heard Jesus say, 'Come to me, all you who are weary and burdened, and I will give you rest' (*Matt 11:28*).

There is, however, one essential difference in the assurance that is ours, in contrast to the fears of the disciples in the Upper Room on the eve of the crucifixion. The disciples thought they were going to lose the presence of their master. But we know that we have his presence in the person of the Holy Spirit – forever!

Prayer
Holy Spirit, help us
Daily, by thy might.
(William Henry Parker, SASB 193)

SUNDAY 10 JUNE
The Spirit's Desires

Romans 8:5–17

'Those who live in accordance with the Spirit have their minds set on what the Spirit desires' (v. 5b, NIV).

That text is a one-sentence summary of the teachings in this Pentecost series – so living in accordance with the Spirit that we seek to live day by day with our minds set on what the Spirit desires.

The desire of the Holy Spirit is that we know the fullness of his presence in our lives, with every compartment of our being open to his control, nothing held back. And that means:

- relying not on our weakness but on the Spirit's power;
- seeking for the impurities of our lives to be purged by the fire of the Holy Spirit so that the Spirit's purity pervades our every impulse;
- discovering and developing our gifts and committing them to God's purposes so that they are indeed the Spirit's gifts;
- allowing the Spirit's fruit of love to be the primary motivation of our lives;
- being sensitive to the Spirit's guidance whatever the cost;
- and knowing the Spirit's comfort as the constant presence of the living Christ being called alongside to be our help.

Life's experiences, however, affirm the pull of our minds also being set on what our sinful nature desires (*Rom 8:5*). Consequently, this side of seeing Jesus face to face, there are failures in our sensitivity to the Spirit and what he wills. But when we fall, he can lift us up and walk alongside us in our journey, so that we do indeed walk in the Spirit, with each step leading us closer to having our minds set on living in accordance with his desires.

Prayer

Come, Holy Ghost, all sacred fire!
  Come, fill this earthly temple now
Emptied of every base desire,
  Reign thou within, and only thou.

Fill every chamber of my soul;
  Fill all my thoughts, my passions fill,
Till under thy supreme control
  Submissive rests my cheerful will.
        (Francis Bottome, SASB 208)

INTRODUCTION TO 1 JOHN
Knowing You, Jesus

A modern-day author, Brennan Manning, says, 'The greatest single need in the church is to know Jesus Christ.'[2] The apostle John would agree. Now aged, John writes with a tender, fatherly tone to believers, his 'little children', to dispel the doubts that have been spread abroad by false teachers, and to build faith by presenting a clear picture of Christ.

John writes from a privileged perspective. As one of Jesus's earliest followers, John had walked and talked with Jesus, seen him heal, heard him teach, watched him die, met him arisen and seen him ascend. John 'knew' him, and he writes to pass on the certainties that he has witnessed at first hand.

In striking yet simple language he presents God as light, as love and as life. He explains in strong and practical terms what it means to have fellowship with God, and with his Son, Jesus Christ.

This letter contains a clear word for believers today. When so much is changing around us, we need to be reminded of the unchanging truths that stand rock-like in our journey of faith. In our dark world, God brings light. In our cold world, God brings the warmth of his love. In our dying world, God brings life.

May the reading of these certainties overwhelm you with God's love and bring renewed confidence to your faith. Knowing him, you can then make him known.

> *Knowing you, Jesus, knowing you, there is no greater thing.*
> *You're my all, you're the best, you're my joy, my righteousness*
> *And I love you, Lord.*
>
> Graham Kendrick, *'All I once held dear'*[3]

MONDAY 11 JUNE
A Credible Witness

1 John 1:1–4

'That which was from the beginning, which we have heard, which we have seen with our eyes, which we have looked at and our hands have touched – this we proclaim concerning the Word of life' (v. 1, NIV).

By the time John wrote this letter, probably between AD 85 and 90, he was an old man, perhaps the only surviving apostle. He had not yet been banished to the island of Patmos where he would live out his last days in exile.

His greatest credential for writing this letter is that he himself was an eyewitness of Christ. He was present at the beginning of Jesus's ministry, being one of the first disciples to be called (*Mark 1:19,20*), and was there at the very end, standing by the cross with Jesus's mother as her son died. And so John writes authoritatively of what he has seen, heard, touched and known. All his senses have been engaged in this relationship.

He says he has seen Christ with his own eyes (*v. 1*). His was no passing glance, but a long searching gaze of wondering love that has discovered something of the meaning of the mystery of Christ. This is the same John who wrote, 'We beheld his glory' (*John 1:14, AV*), or to put it another way, 'We saw the glory with our own eyes' (*The Message*).

John heard him speak – to children, crowds and corpses, on mountaintops and in lonely gardens. One of Jesus's inner circle, known as 'the disciple Jesus loved', John not only heard Jesus's words, but felt his very heartbeat as well.

'Our hands have touched him.' In the first verse John challenges the argument of those who were saying that Jesus only 'seemed' to be human, an ethereal figure who cast no shadow and left no footprints. 'I've heard him speak, I've touched him with my own hands, seen him with my own eyes.' These statements are the certainties of an authentic witness.

Even today, no one can deny the power of such a personal witness. 'This is what I know of God. This is how God has revealed himself to me.' When such a claim is backed up by a life of consistent, loving service, then debate and argument are silenced.

To reflect on
Does your witness as a Christian sound credible?

TUESDAY 12 JUNE
An Enemy Within

---
1 John 1:1–4

'We write this to make our joy complete' (v. 4, NIV).

By the time John wrote this letter, Jerusalem had been destroyed (AD 70) and Christians were scattered throughout the Roman Empire. In many places they had suffered severe persecution, but the faith had survived and was being passed on to new believers.

But now a new danger was at hand – not an external enemy this time, but false teachers within the Church itself who were seducing believers from the true faith. They taught that salvation is to be found, not by faith in Christ, but by special mystical knowledge (Greek – *gnosis*). A central belief of Gnosticism was that spirit is good but matter is evil. Thus the world and the human body in particular are evil.

So they considered that it was impossible that God could ever clothe himself with human flesh. Jesus simply 'seemed' to have a body, but he was in fact a pure spiritual being. This view is called Docetism from the Greek *dokeo*, 'to seem'. Furthermore, others said that the divine Christ joined the man Jesus at his baptism and left him before he died.

The effect of this insidious teaching was to entice believers away from their faith in the human, living, dying, resurrected Jesus. Commitment was declining, people were failing to stand up for their faith, compromise was happening. A cooling-off of faith was resulting in a lukewarm, half-hearted Church.

Who better to speak a word of certainty and encouragement to believers than one who was certain himself of what he had seen and heard of the living Jesus? To these teachers who claimed to have 'special knowledge', John writes strongly, unashamedly, joyfully of what he has known of the living Lord.

To reflect on
'We saw it, we heard it, and now we're telling you so you can experience it along with us, this experience of communion with the Father and his Son, Jesus Christ. Our motive for writing is simply this: We want you to enjoy this, too. Your joy will double our joy!'

(The Message)

WEDNESDAY 13 JUNE
God Is Light

1 John 1:5–7

'This is the message we have heard from him and declare to you:
God is light; in him there is no darkness at all' (v. 5, NIV).

John, the pastor, writes to his 'dear children' to teach them about error and to love them into truth. 'God is light,' he writes, 'and there is no darkness in him.' In the first section of John's letter (1:5–3:10) he makes it clear that right thinking about God is essential for life in the Christian community. Walking in the light of God will enable believers to walk in the light with each other.

In using the image of light to describe God, John is using one of his own favourite descriptions. His Gospel features over forty references to light. 'The light shines in the darkness' (John 1:5). 'The true light that gives light to every man, was coming into the world' (John 1:9). Jesus said, 'I am the light of the world' (John 8:12).

Such a description would be understood by the false teachers, for Gnosticism promoted a religion of mystic enlightenment. Cleverly, John picks up the image and subtly issues a word of challenge to those who say they are in the light, but whose actions indicate that they are still living in the darkness.

- God is light – pure, perfect and utterly righteous.
- God's light reveals our spiritual identity – whether we abide in the Son or whether we live in the darkness.
- God's light guides us through the minefield of sin, and out into the safe place of forgiveness and cleansing.
- God's light judges, for it unveils what is hidden deep in our hearts.
- God's light heals as we receive forgiveness and are enabled then to hold out our hand in forgiveness and fellowship to others.
- God's light gives us direction when we do not know where to go.

The light has come! Let the God who is light shine a full beam of his light into your heart today.

To reflect on
The light that shattered the darkness puts together the broken pieces of our lives.
(Written on a Christmas card)

THURSDAY 14 JUNE

If . . .

---
1 John 1:5–10

'If we confess our sins, he is faithful and just and will forgive us our sins and purify us from all unrighteousness' (v. 9, NIV).

'There is no such thing as sin.' 'The subject of sin is old-fashioned, irrelevant, politically incorrect.' 'The body is eventually going to decay, so you might as well gratify every wish, every urge and lust now.'

These statements have a familiar sound in today's society. And so taught the false teachers of John's day. Because the human body was considered evil, there was no such thing as a moral law of right living to be obeyed. 'Dear children,' John writes, with a wistful sadness, 'do not let anyone lead you astray' (3:7). 'If we claim that we're free of sin, we're only fooling ourselves' (*1:8, The Message*). With brevity and masterful use of the word 'if', he confronts some of the Gnostics' false teachings:

1:6 If we claim to have fellowship with him yet walk in the darkness . . .
1:7 But if we walk in the light, as he is in the light . . .

1:8 If we claim to be without sin . . .
1:9 If we confess our sins . . .

The unsettlers in John's church were claiming to have a close walk with God, and that their lives were unstained with sin. They went so far as to claim that the whole question of sin was unimportant and irrelevant because God, who is holy and pure, has nothing to do with the common stuff of life. Not so, says John. A good God expects good people. If we claim to know the God of light, yet are walking in darkness, then we are living a lie. Forgiveness and cleansing are essential, he says, so that God's transforming work can have permanent results in our lives and in the world.

1 John 1:9 is one of the greatest, most reassuring verses of the Scriptures. It is a foundation text for every new Christian and for every believer, at every stage of the journey. If we confess, then he is faithful and just, he will forgive, he will cleanse.

Let this word of forgiveness and full cleansing speak to you today!

FRIDAY 15 JUNE

Fellowship

1 John 1:3–4

'Our fellowship is with the Father and with his Son, Jesus Christ'
(v. 3, NIV).

On a recent holiday, we attended a Sunday morning worship service arranged by seven churches in the city. The large town hall was packed to capacity. The atmosphere was thrilling, the singing heavenly. The following week, we found ourselves among a little group of worshippers – just fifteen in all. The atmosphere was subdued, the singing something of a strain. But it was still church – the gathering of God's people to worship and celebrate the resurrected Lord.

One of John's favourite words is 'fellowship' (1 John 1:3,6,7), translated from the Greek word *koinonia* which means to have something in common. In fact, it is one of his reasons for writing this letter, to remind his readers of the precious gift of oneness with others that comes when we walk in oneness with God.

Christian community is not just some passing association of people who share common interests, like pet-lovers or weavers. Nor is it an intellectual group where discussion about issues to do with God makes people appreciate each other. It is far deeper than these things. It is the common living of people who have a shared experience of Jesus Christ.

This Christian fellowship is like a triangle: my life in fellowship with Christ, your life in fellowship with Christ, and my life in fellowship with yours. The mystical union we enjoy with Christ binds the Church together.

We are the Church – a divine creation (God's idea) and a human institution (made up of people). While conflict and struggle are inevitable, the hallmarks of this community should be love (see *John 13:34,35*), fellowship and joy (v. 4).

It is a wonderful experience to be visiting another country and to recognise another Christian – by a book they are reading, a bumper sticker, a chorus whistled, or a similar response to a sudden need. 'Hallelujah' may be the only word that is shared, but something of the Spirit of God in each other is caught and understood.

To reflect on
As Christians, the things we hold in common are greater than the differences that separate us.

SATURDAY 16 JUNE
'My Dear Children'

1 John 2:12–14

'I write to you, young men, because you are strong, and the word of God lives in you, and you have overcome the evil one' (v. 14, NIV).

As I lean over John's shoulder to read what he is writing, I discover, to my surprise, that he is writing to me, and to you. Even more surprising is the tone with which he writes. With the tender love of a spiritual father, he addresses his readers – 'My dear children' (2:1,12, 28) and 'dear friends' (2:7, 3:2,21).

John tackles some tough issues – heresies in the Church, who Jesus is, the tests of true faith, the question of sin – but his tone is unfailingly warm and gracious. There is no scolding here, no impatient irritability with wandering believers, no cutting criticism. Just the tender-hearted affection of a pastor who has lived a long time and, with the discernment of an elder statesman, sees what is happening to his beloved church. At the time of writing, John may have been the last survivor of his generation, maybe the last man alive who had walked and talked with the human Jesus.

'I'm writing to you, dear children', he says, 'to remind you that your sins have been forgiven in Jesus's name.'

'I'm writing to you, veterans of the faith, to remind you of all you've been taught over the years.'

'I'm writing to you, newcomers, to remind you that your strength and vitality will come only from your close fellowship with God.'

These three categories of people – children, veterans and newcomers – may well have been groups of people within the church. But if we look deeper into John's words, we realise that at every age and stage we all need the blessings that he writes of – the reminder of forgiveness, the importance of holding fast to the truth we know, and God as the source of our strength and victory.

This letter then, so full of tender love, is written to you, believer, no matter how old you are in your experience of God. May you be reminded again today of God's forgiveness, of the truth you have been taught, and that he is the source of your strength.

To reflect on
I am the one Jesus loves.

SUNDAY 17 JUNE
An Evening Prayer

Psalm 4

'Answer me when I call to you, O my righteous God' (v. 1, NIV).

I woke as a scratching sound jolted me out of deep sleep. What was that? The cat clawing at a window? No, the cat wouldn't make that much noise. I quietly got up, walked along the passage and into the front room. I pulled back the curtain just as two men lifted the security screen away from the window. Shocked, I yelled at them. My sudden ghostly appearance in a white nightgown shocked them too! They dropped the screen and ran. My dear husband slept through it all, but murmured, 'What was that?' as I climbed back into bed, shaking.

A break-in had been averted, but that scene replayed itself in my mind every night for the next few months. I would awaken suddenly and lie there, straining to hear what had woken me. Tired, stressed and unsleeping, I asked God for a verse to help me, and he led me to Psalm 4:8: 'I will lie down and sleep in peace, for you alone, O LORD, make me dwell in safety.' Gradually the verse did its work. I was able to rest, knowing that God who keeps the night watch (*Ps 121:4*) would keep me safe.

More dramatically, the psalmist came to the same place of peace and rest. Psalm 4 begins amidst oppression, distress and false accusations, and concludes with peaceful confidence in God. External circumstances may not have changed. The accusations were presumably still there, prodding like barbs in his mind. But he has found an answer. Prayer has led him to a calmness of mind that also gives rest to his body.

There are many things that can keep us lying awake – anxiety about health, work or finances, distress over loved family members, conflict and uncertainty about a host of concerns. But God is always in control, even through the night. He invites us to lay our burdens before him as we lie down to sleep. May we receive from him the same peace and quiet confidence the psalmist found.

Pray for those who suffer from insomnia – that the burden-bearing God will give them rest.

MONDAY 18 JUNE

God Is Love

1 John 4:7–8

'Whoever does not love does not know God, because God is love' (v. 8, NIV).

In these three small words, 'God is love', John makes a statement that reaches higher, deeper, wider, further than the whole universe. From 4:7 to 5:3 the word 'love' is used thirty-two times. This isn't love as in 'I love jam sandwiches' or 'I love going to the movies'. This is love that describes the very being and nature of God. Just as he wrote in his Gospel that God is spirit (*John 4:24*) and previously in this letter that God is light (*1:5*), so now John writes of God who, in his essential nature and in all his actions, is loving.

These things we can say of love:

- Love has its origin, its beginning point in God (*v. 7*). When it comes to love, God is the great initiator. When we love, we are bearing 'the beams of his love'.
- Love is a two-way relationship with God. It is only by knowing God that we learn to love, and only by loving that we learn to know God (*vv. 7,8*).
- It is by love that God is known (*v. 12*). A young Asian woman, brought up in a deprived and harsh environment, spoke of a Christian friend, Alice, who had led her to faith in Jesus. 'I never knew that God loved me,' she said, 'until I met Alice.'
- God's love is demonstrated to us in Jesus Christ (*v. 9*). It is in Jesus that we see a sacrificial love that has held nothing back.
- Our human love is a response to the initiative of God's love (*v. 19*). It is not a product of the human heart, but a response to God's love.
- Like a triangle whose points are God, self and others, God's love for us and our love for others are inseparably linked (*vv. 7,11,20,21*).

These are some of the strong statements that John had in his heart as he wrote to his 'beloved children'.

To reflect on

May we, as God's beloved children today, have our eyes open to all the expressions of God's love around us.

TUESDAY 19 JUNE
God's Lavish Love

1 John 3:1–3

'How great is the love the Father has lavished on us, that we should be called children of God! And that is what we are!' (v. 1, NIV).

A couple came one Sunday to conduct the meeting where my husband and I were the corps officers. At lunch afterwards, my children watched with widening eyes as one of our guests plopped spoonfuls of whipped cream onto his dessert. Lavish was his dessert, piled high was the cream, great was his delight!

I think of that man every time I read this verse from 1 John 3. God has lavished his love on us, more and more. Surely one measure of it would be enough, but no, he keeps adding more and more, and yet more. There's only one word for this kind of love, and that's 'extravagant'! Have you ever thought of God as a 'lavish, extravagant lover'?

John tells his readers that God's love has been poured out upon us lavishly because he delights to call us his children. His love gives us our identity as members of his family. 'And that is exactly who we really are!' he affirms. That's a 'now' experience (v. 1), not something stored away for a needy day sometime in the future, like an insurance policy.

But we are also in a process of becoming (v. 2). If now we have a glimpse of what it means to have the presence of the Father within us, when Christ comes there will be even more overwhelming experiences of his love for us. He will appear, we will appear just like him, and then we will see him exactly as he is. In that day there will be an immediate and unmistakable unity between us and the Father.

All this and heaven too! But to describe it fully is impossible. Paul wrote, 'No eye has seen, no ear has heard, no mind has conceived what God has prepared for those who love him' (1 Cor 2:9). What is being set in place for us in the future sounds even more lavish and extravagant!

To reflect on
What would your life look like if you knew you were lavishly, extravagantly loved?

WEDNESDAY 20 JUNE
Do You Pass the Test?

1 John 2:28–29; 4:20–21

'He has given us this command: Whoever loves God must also love his brother' (4:21, NIV).

'When I was going through a difficult time in my life, about ten years ago,' a woman wrote to her friend, 'you helped me so much. I knew you were a woman who knew God.' What an amazing and humbling thing to be told! On what basis did that person in need consider that her friend 'knew' God? Is there a test for knowing, a tick-list of characteristics?

- Humble? – yes.
- Generous? – well, sometimes.
- Available? – most days . . .

John writes that there are indeed two tests for those who claim to know God. There's the righteousness test, and then there's the love test (also known as the obedience test).

John writes strongly. 'Once you're convinced that [God] is right and righteous, you'll recognize that all who practice righteousness are God's true children' (2:29, *The Message*). There's a power of authenticity, magnetism and confidence about someone who knows God and who lives out the certainty of that relationship. And it doesn't have to be loud to be noticed!

John says the other proof that we love God is the keeping of his commandment to love others. The Gnostics, with their teaching of spiritual enlightenment that was kept for the privileged few, would have said that the mark of true religion is contempt for ordinary people. John insists in every chapter of this letter that the mark of true religion is love for all others.

The absence of love for one another, he says, reveals an absence of love for God. Those who live with this double standard, saying that they love God but in their hearts hate some human being, are, in John's unashamed words, 'liars'. 'The one who won't practice righteous ways isn't from God, nor is the one who won't love brother or sister. A simple test' (3:10, *The Message*).

To reflect on
Do you pass this love test today? It's a helpful experience to make a list of those who have hurt or wronged us, and then to pray them out of enemies and into friends.

THURSDAY 21 JUNE
Give Him His Rightful Place

1 John 4:9–16

'This is love: not that we loved God, but that he loved us and sent his Son as an atoning sacrifice for our sins' (v. 10, NIV).

In countering the false teachers' claims about the human body being evil, John goes right to the heart of the matter – Jesus. Right thinking about Jesus will result in right theology, which will result in right living.

John is not writing abstract doctrine about Jesus. Rather, he emphasises that, at a specific moment in time, he who had existed from limitless eternity entered time and space and took up residence here on earth. Jesus was the Word of God incarnate, the very expression of God in human flesh. These words echo the beginning of John's Gospel, 'In the beginning was the Word, and the Word was with God, and the Word was God.' With his own eyes, ears and hands, John has watched him, listened and talked to him, touched him. John has known him so closely that he can speak with authority, giving 'the inside story', the authentic eyewitness account.

In strong statements, John writes that the coming of Jesus in human form, his life, death, resurrection and ascension, all work together to deal with the sin of mankind. Although he himself was sinless (3:5), he came at God's loving initiative and plan to deal with our sin. As our advocate (2:1) he defends us, pleading our case with God. Even more, he is the atoning sacrifice for our sins (2:2; 4:10). Into the relationship between humanity and God that was severed by sin, Jesus has come, bearing the punishment of sin in our place, setting us 'at one' again with God, and cleansing us through and through.

Whether these truths are startlingly new to you today, believer, or old and familiar, let the wonder of what Jesus has done fill your heart once again. Whenever we sing 'Ransomed, healed, restored, forgiven' (*SASB* 17), I feel like standing on a box to sing. Find yourself a box today, stand tall on it and lift your heart in worship to this:

Life-bringing (4:9)
  Relationship-restoring (4:10)
    Saviour of the world (4:14)
      Son of God (4:15)
        Our Lord Jesus Christ!

FRIDAY 22 JUNE

God Is Life

---
1 John 5:11–12

'This is the testimony: God has given us eternal life, and this life is in his Son' (v. 11, NIV).

Our family holidays, when I was growing up, were usually spent at a seaside town, Riverton Rocks, about two hours' drive from home. There we swam, walked the beach and hunted for crabs in the rock pools. It was also there, every year, that my sister and I joined in with CSSM – Children's Special Service Mission, a Christian outreach to families on holiday.

I recall one year being given key Scripture passages for young Christians, and among them were verses from 1 John 5. I was intrigued by the words. I was captivated by their contrast (having life and not having life), by their certainty (the strong repeated use of 'has') and by the centrality of Jesus to the whole matter. Somehow he was the key to this question of eternal life. Those words began for me a journey of exploration into what it means to have Jesus and to have eternal life.

These words at the end of John's letter are a summary of what he has written and a statement of the greatest certainty we can have. It is not a 'hope-so' gospel, but a 'know-so'. As Christians we do not have to wait for eternal life – it has already begun. It begins for us when we receive Jesus into our lives. We do not have to work for it, because it is already ours, gifted to us and wrapped up in Jesus. We do not need to worry about it, because we have been given eternal life by God himself, and it has a heaven-backed guarantee.

To a seeking child, a gift that didn't need to be waited for, worked for or worried about was worth having. Now, as an adult enjoying some of the fruits of the eternal life relationship which began for me that year at Riverton Rocks, I find that gift means more than everything.

To reflect on
Have you received the gift of eternal life that God offers you in Jesus? It doesn't need to be your birthday or Christmas for you to accept this gift today!

SATURDAY 23 JUNE

Certainties

1 John 5:13–20

'I write these things to you who believe in the name of the Son of God so that you may know that you have eternal life' (v. 13, NIV).

The word 'know' is sprinkled liberally throughout this last chapter of John's letter to believers, his 'dear children' (v. 21), as he concludes with a list of certainties. This is his final word of encouragement.

John understands the world of his readers and all the forces lined up against them, both inside and outside the Church, but he is convinced that their faith does not need to lack assurance (v. 13). Modern-day prophets say that change and uncertainty are all we can be sure of, but John speaks of certainties. He reminds his readers and us that Christ has not only worked on our behalf (v. 20), but he also protects us from habitual sinning (v. 18). God's commitment is such that he listens to our prayers (v. 14) and has guaranteed us eternal life (v. 13). Jesus sustains us in the midst of the disintegration of the world. Our believing and living as Christians must come out of the deep knowing of these truths.

A young woman spoke of her dismay at the Church, although she had not attended a service for some years. 'It is so hard to believe the things about Jesus when his followers behave as they do,' she said. The word 'hypocrisy' was not far from her lips. If this young woman had been speaking to John, he would have told her, 'Jesus is true even though all else fails. You are still a child of God even though your family, the Church, is broken. And you can still discover the light and walk in it, even if those around you are giving in to the darkness.'

May John's certainties be our certainties today!

If our darkened eyes could see him,
If our sight could be restored,
We would know that he walks with us,
Glimpse the glory of the Lord.
We would recognise his handprints,
Trace his footsteps on our road,
We would see his love in action,
Feel his strong arm lift our load.

Open my eyes to see Jesus,
Speak your certainties deep within,
With love that's unfailing and truth
that's unchanging,
Open my eyes to see him.

(Barbara Sampson)

SUNDAY 24 JUNE
A Morning Prayer

Psalm 5

'In the morning, O LORD, you hear my voice; in the morning I lay my requests before you and wait in expectation' (v. 3, NIV).

Psalm 5 is a prayer for the morning. Like the psalmist, we stretch our limbs and prepare for the day by lifting our heart to God. 'Give ear... consider... listen... for to you I pray' (vv. 1,2). God will hear, not because we are so skilled in asking, but because he is God.

The psalmist knew – and we know too – that the daylight world of activity is full of danger and demand, conflict and choice. This day, like all days, will be full of words – godly words and ungodly words. Words of boasters and evildoers (vv. 5,6) will mix with words of worshippers and pilgrims (vv. 7,8). Liars and deceivers (vv. 9,10) will mingle with singers and lovers (vv. 11,12).

It seems the psalmist knew mankind and himself well enough to know that the words of mockers and deceivers were not just sounds from the enemy out there. He could no doubt identify those who were trying to bring him down with their lies and curses. But even as he prays, he knows that the enemy also lurks within, and he will need protection from his own potentially evil tongue.

And so he prays, 'I lay my requests before you and wait in expectation.' He chooses to worship. 'I will come', he says with determination, knowing that in God's presence there will be a refuge. In offering himself like a sacrifice, he is laying before God full ownership and control, and waiting to see what God will do.

The invitation that comes to us, modern-day pilgrims, is to do the same. To lay before God each morning the colourful, crazy assortment of words, activities and possibilities of the day as it stretches before us, and to see where he will take us. The night has passed. The new day is full of dangers, but a covering of angel wings protects us (v. 11) as we set our hearts upon God once again and move out into the day.

Prayer
'May the words of my mouth and the meditation of my heart be pleasing in your sight, O LORD' (Ps 19:14).

INTRODUCTION TO MARK 1–3
Who Is This Man?

As we launch into a four-week series of readings from the first three chapters of Mark's Gospel, we inevitably get drawn into a story that is full of colour, sound and activity. We see a rapid succession of pictures of Jesus in action, in full Technicolor. This is Jesus on the move, refusing to be contained or controlled, his true identity revealed by what he does, as much as by what he says.

We watch intimate moments of baptism and temptation, and then his public ministry begins as he confronts demons, heals the sick, forgives those who are paralysed in more ways than one. And as his fame spreads, so does the opposition from religious leaders who are both fascinated and furious with him.

In almost every conversation or encounter, an unspoken question hovers in the air – Who is this man? He doesn't fit the stereotype of Messiah that people were expecting. Unlike other religious leaders who kept sinners at arm's length, this man throws his arms around them. Old Zebedee, the father of James and John, must have wondered who Jesus was when he came along and whisked his sons away from the family fishing business *(1:20)*. The man whose ceiling was broken through must have pondered that question, as much as the paralysed man at the centre of Jesus' healing attention that day *(2:1-12)*. Even Jesus's own family wondered just who he was as they came to take him away *(3:21)*.

It's a question for us also, perhaps the most important question we will ever ask – Who are you, Lord? It's a question with a catch to it, for our answer demands a commitment. C. S. Lewis said that when we are faced with Jesus's claims, we have only two options – either he is a madman, or he is the Son of God.[4]

If he is the former, we can try to silence him, as others did. But if he is the Son of God, then we too must fall at his feet and call him Lord.

MONDAY 25 JUNE
Mark's Gospel

Mark 1:1

'The beginning of the gospel about Jesus Christ, the Son of God' (v. 1, NIV).

Mark's Gospel is an action-packed recording of Jesus' life and death. Mark was not one of the twelve disciples, but his Gospel is the closest we have to an eyewitness account, as it is believed to be the record of the apostle Peter's preaching. There is so much similar material in Matthew and Luke's Gospels that it is believed that they, writing later than Mark, drew heavily upon his account. Mark records more of Jesus's miracles than his sermons, painting Jesus clearly as a man of power and action, not just words.

Most of the stories are told in the order in which they occurred. Mark writes simply, succinctly and vividly, moving quickly from one episode in Jesus' life and ministry to another. His favourite words seem to be 'immediately' or 'at once'. There are no superfluous words or details. He tells the story as an eager child would tell it, with statement after statement connected simply with the word 'and'. He rushes the story on in a breathless attempt to tell it as vividly as it has been told to him.

But in the midst of frenetic activity, he shows Jesus always with a deep sense of purpose. He is caught up in a rising tide of events and opposition, and yet always seems to be majestically in charge. He seems never to be still, yet always to have time. His intense activity is nourished and grounded in moments of silence.

Mark could well be the patron saint of all who are in a tearing hurry. Certainly he is a man for our times with a message for our times, when there seems never to be enough time – for that relationship to be built, that book to be read, that person to be cared for, that task to be done.

To reflect on

As we hurry with Mark into his account of Jesus, may we find our harried step slowing to keep time with the Lord's measured pace. May our frenetic activity be slowed as we glimpse the deep, calm sense of purpose that Jesus bore.

TUESDAY 26 JUNE
The Beginning of the Good News

Mark 1:1

'The beginning of the gospel about Jesus Christ, the Son of God'
(v. 1, NIV).

The opening of Mark's Gospel (1:1) is as abrupt as its ending (16:8). 'The beginning of the good news of Jesus Christ, the Son of God.' This statement without a verb serves as a title for the whole Gospel (1:2–16:8), telling us right at the start what this work is about.

The whole Gospel is about a beginning. But it is a beginning without an ending. In 16:8 the women flee from the tomb, trembling with fear and saying nothing to anyone. Mark does not finish the story because the announcement of Jesus's resurrection and his going before his disciples to Galilee is not the final stage. The story of the gospel of Jesus Christ continues to be told, and will be told 'till the end of time and to the ends of the earth' (cf. 13:10; 14:9). We who read these words are part of a great beginning, initiated by God, and yet to be concluded.

God is a God of beginnings. This Gospel and our lives seem to be made up of hellos and goodbyes, beginnings and endings and new beginnings. The fear and failure and gloom of the last verses of Mark's Gospel are not the end of the story. The disciples had scattered (14:50), Peter had denied Jesus (14:71), the women were struck dumb with fear. How could these dismayed disciples emerge as leaders of a vibrant, growing Church and fulfil their mission? It seems like an ending, but really it is a new beginning. Their failure was not final, and neither is ours.

God is the one who consistently, lovingly makes something out of nothing. God continues today to work with and revive his people. Mark makes it clear that the Church exists because of what God has done in Christ, not because of any outstanding abilities in its first members. Paul proclaims that the one 'who began a good work in you will carry it on to completion until the day of Christ Jesus' (Phil 1:6).

To reflect on
God welcomes you to a new beginning today!

WEDNESDAY 27 JUNE
A Signpost of a Man

Mark 1:2–8

'So John came, baptising in the desert region and preaching a baptism of repentance for the forgiveness of sins' (v. 4, NIV).

In the far south of New Zealand a signpost stands, giving the distances to far-off cities. London – 19,000 km; New York – 15,000 km; Sydney – 2,000 km. Tourists flock to have their photographs taken there. No one comes to admire the signpost itself – 'Long and tall, set in concrete, yellow with black writing'. They come to see where the signpost points.

John the Baptist was a signpost, pointing to Jesus. Mark plunges us into the story. Important Roman officials of his day were always preceded by an announcer or herald. Mark, writing to Roman Christians, begins with John the Baptist, the one whose mission it was to announce the coming of Jesus. A voice from off-stage reads the promise-filled words of Isaiah, showing that while John and Jesus may seem to appear out of the blue, they in fact appear out of the blueprint of God's plan. This is the beginning of the good news, but it began a long time before John emerged.

Mark tells us none of the background details about John that we find in Luke's Gospel – his origin, parents, marvellous birth, or the contents of his teaching. Mark simply describes his clothing and food. He appears tall, lean and eccentric, like a resurrected Elijah, standing out against the religious leaders of the day, whose long, flowing robes reflected their great pride in their position. His striking appearance reinforces his remarkable message of repentance. John's task is to announce the coming of the more powerful one. His baptism would drench them in water, but that was only in preparation for the one coming who would drench them in the Holy Spirit.

Although John was the first genuine prophet in 400 years, Jesus the Messiah would be infinitely greater than he. John pointed out how insignificant he was compared to the one who was coming. He was not even worthy of untying his sandals. What John began, Jesus finished. What John prepared, Jesus fulfilled.

To reflect on
John comes as a voice crying, a lowly servant.
Jesus comes as the beloved Son, the suffering Servant.

THURSDAY 28 JUNE
A Holy Moment

Mark 1: 9–11

'A voice came from heaven: "You are my Son, whom I love; with you I am well pleased." ' (v. 11, NIV).

Jesus's arrival on the scene at the River Jordan is something of an anticlimax after such a graphic introduction. He comes, not as a conquering Messiah, but as a submissive Messiah. To the disappointment of many, sensational public displays are not going to be a feature of his ministry. With no special aura or halo to distinguish him from the rest of the crowd, he simply comes and lines up for baptism.

Jesus is the sinless one, with no need of repentance, but this action launches his ministry and affirms John in his. In humility Jesus identifies with our humanness and sin. What might he have said to his cousin as he let himself be plunged in the Jordan? 'I need this too, John!' Mark, unlike Matthew (*Matt 3:14*), does not record John as making any protest.

When Jesus comes up out of the water, heaven opens. God is now in our midst. The hope of Isaiah, 'Oh, that you would rend the heavens and come down, that the mountains would tremble before you!' (*Isa 64:1*) has come to pass. The power from heaven that commences Jesus's ministry does not swoop down like an eagle or a falcon but descends quietly and gently, like a dove.

As a powerful reminder of the hovering of the Spirit of God over the primeval waters in the beginning of time (*Gen 1:2*), this dove-like hovering of the Spirit on Jesus is a sign that God's new creation, the transformation of humanity has begun. A voice from the sundered heavens sounds out, 'You are my Son, whom I love; with you I am well pleased.' At the very beginning of his ministry, Jesus is assured that he is beloved by words of approval spoken directly to him. We eavesdrop on holy ground as we read Mark's words and realise the presence of the Trinity – Father, Son and Holy Spirit – in this scene by the Jordan.

To reflect on
Father, you called Jesus 'my beloved Son'. What name do you call me today?

FRIDAY 29 JUNE
A Battle to End All Battles

Mark 1:12-13

'At once the Spirit sent him out into the desert . . .' (v. 12, NIV).

Jesus moves from the sacred moment of the Spirit's descent and the affirmation that he is beloved, to the harshness of Satan's temptations in the wilderness. The Spirit is present in both movements – the Spirit descended (v. 10) and the Spirit drove (v. 12). The baptism is no sooner over than the battle begins.

How often a high spiritual moment seems to be eclipsed by a time of testing. It is almost a spiritual principle that the higher the moment, the harsher and faster the comedown from it. Jesus shows his humanity in being, like us, subject to this spiritual reality (see Heb 4:15).

For the inside story of these temptations, we need to read Matthew or Luke's account. Mark simply tells us who the main players were – Jesus and Satan. The desert is a barren place and the wild beasts add to the picture of desolation and danger. For forty days the battle rages, his only comfort the angels who come to attend to him.

Whether this is a once-and-for-all decisive victory, and Jesus's encounters with demons during his ministry simply a mopping-up after the battle, or whether this is merely the first round in Jesus's struggle against evil, we are not told. One thing is clear. The appearance of the Son of God is a direct onslaught on Satan's realm. All the unclean spirits Jesus will encounter in his ministry recognise him and cower before him. The exorcisms he performs prove that the powerful one, Satan, has been bound by an even more powerful one (Mark 3:22–27), and that his house can now be cleaned out. When Jesus encounters demons, the outcome is never in doubt.

The temptation, like the baptism, has cosmic significance. This is a power struggle between Jesus, the Son of God, and the Prince of the forces of evil. The power of God, long promised, breaks into the world in the person of Jesus to conquer the powers of evil that imprison, maim and distort human life.

To reflect on
Lift up your head to the coming king!

SATURDAY 30 JUNE
In His Time

Mark 1:14–15

'The time has come,' he said. 'The kingdom of God is near.
Repent and believe the good news!' (v. 15, NIV).

Jesus's clash with Satan in the wilderness clearly does not end in a tie. The preaching of the good news of God that immediately follows is the proclamation of victory. The world is now under new government!

And so Jesus comes, Mark tells us, after John is arrested. John seems to be suddenly dismissed but he is more than a town crier, announcing the coming of a great king and then disappearing. He is Jesus's forerunner in his ministry to Israel, in his fateful conflict with earthly authorities, and in his brutal death.

After John's arrest, Jesus comes to Galilee. The beginning of Jesus's ministry anchors him in a specific moment in history and in a specific place. This is 'chronos' time, as Luke fixes it so accurately. 'In the fifteenth year of the reign of Tiberius Caesar – when Pontius Pilate was governor of Judea, Herod tetrarch of Galilee ... during the high priesthood of Annas and Caiaphas ...' (Luke 3:1–2). It is also 'kairos' time – time seen from God's side. Jesus makes his appearance when the time is fulfilled (see Gal 4:4). The kingdom of God is at hand. It is here, in the person of Jesus.

And he requires a response. The announcement that the King and his kingdom are at hand contains a demand for an immediate human decision and commitment.

A young man I know spent years of his life in drugs and alcohol. He worked in order to drink and party. But one morning, a few years after his wife's life-changing conversion, he was awakened by an insistent inner voice: 'Get up and go to the Salvation Army.' Surprised, he did, and on that very day was himself converted and welcomed into the kingdom. It was God's 'kairos' time – a moment that God had known and planned from the beginning of time (Eph 1:4). That couple now serve God as Salvation Army officers.

To reflect on
Whatever time you read these words, would today be God's 'kairos' time for you, a moment of invitation to serve him in a new way?

SUNDAY 1 JULY
Prayer for a Waiting-Room

Psalm 6

'My soul is in anguish. How long, O LORD, how long?' (v. 3, NIV).

Psalm 6 is the first of seven 'penitential' psalms, songs of lament, which were traditionally sung on Ash Wednesday. Feeble because of illness, the psalmist says his bones and his soul are in agony. This is a picture of both physical and spiritual disturbance. 'Don't be angry with me, Lord,' he cries, 'but please be gracious.' Unable to bear the suffering, he pleads for the undeserved but deeply needed grace of God. 'How long, O Lord, how long?'

His words have a tragically familiar ring to them. How many believers these days know from the inside the agonising depths of that prayer! 'How long, Lord, do I have to wait for my loved one to be healed?' 'How long, Lord, do we as parents have to wait for our prodigal child to come home?' 'How long, Lord, do I have to wait for my marriage to be restored, that relationship to be mended, that overwhelming grief to ease?' 'How long, Lord, how long?' This is the prayer of the waiting-room, uttered by all who know the dark and lonely place of being able to do nothing but wait for God's answer.

'Turn,' (v. 4) begs the psalmist, 'please come back from what seems like your desertion of me, and hear my prayer once again.' His sickness has created both insomnia and exhaustion. His bed is flooded with tears; his eyes, once bright and clear, are now wasting and weak (v. 7). He has no physical, emotional or spiritual reserves left. He is haunted by the gathering shadows of death.

But then the tone of his prayer suddenly lifts and his confidence returns. God has heard and accepted his prayer. The evil-doers who kept him bound in grief are firmly dismissed. In his new-found confidence, he knows that God will answer and, what's more, those who taunted and shamed him will find their own sin come back upon themselves.

Pray today for someone you know who is in a dark and lonely place, waiting for God's healing answer.

MONDAY 2 JULY
Captured by a Holy Calling

Mark 1:16–20

'As Jesus walked beside the Sea of Galilee, he saw Simon and his brother Andrew casting a net into the lake, for they were fishermen' (v. 16, NIV).

The early morning sun glistened on the still water. Shrieking gulls circled overhead, looking for titbits from the night's fishing trip. Friendly banter from the fishermen tidying up after the night's excursion indicated it had been a good catch. Into this scene of everyday activity walked Jesus. It's time for him to gather his team about him, to create a community of followers.

Peter and Andrew were casting nets from the shoreline, while the Zebedee brothers were in the family boat with their father and the hired hands. No conversation with these prospective followers is recorded, no competency test, no psychological profile. Just a seeing, and a calling. Jesus 'saw Simon and his brother Andrew' (v. 16), and Jesus 'saw James ... and his brother John' (v. 19).

What he saw with those divinely human eyes, we can only guess. The potential in these men? The task that they were doing which fitted them perfectly for a greater task? The companionship and the cross that they would experience together?

Whatever it was Jesus saw, he called them to follow, not a set of beliefs, nor a theological system, but him. This in itself was a striking departure from the norm. Rabbis of Jesus's day did not call people to follow them, but only to learn Torah (the law – the first five books of the Old Testament). Jesus's call, in contrast, is authoritative and personal – 'Follow me.' This command is followed by a promise, 'I will make...' and they respond with what seems to be immediate obedience. This holy calling is so momentous that their lives will never be the same again.

For Percy Smith, a young New Zealander in the 1920s, God's calling was just as momentous. It came through a picture hanging in the local scout den, inscribed 'This is our Lord. He is the Great Pathfinder.' Percy responded, 'You lead the way, I will follow,' and he went on to become a renowned Salvation Army officer in his country.

To reflect on
God sees, he calls, he equips.

TUESDAY 3 JULY
Man of Authority

Mark 1:21–28

'The people were amazed at his teaching, because he taught them as one who had authority, not as the teachers of the law' (v. 22, NIV).

These verses describe the launching of Jesus's campaign in the place where it seems most logical for him to begin – the synagogue. Wherever there were ten Jewish families together, there had to be a synagogue. It was a place of teaching and instruction. A synagogue service had three aspects – prayer, the reading of God's word and exposition of the word. There was no music, singing or sacrifice. Officials worked at the synagogue but there was no paid preacher or teacher. When the people met together for the service, the ruler of the synagogue would call on any competent person to bring the teaching.

Thus Jesus opens his ministry in the company of God's people. He is known to be a man with a message, so he has a ready-made pulpit.

The people hear him with amazement, for he speaks with an authority that is new to them. The scribes who normally taught in the service expounded on the endless rules and regulations they had extracted from the Torah. They would always begin 'There is a teaching that...' But when Jesus speaks, he quotes no experts. He speaks as if he needs no authority beyond himself. He speaks with the finality of the voice of God. That note of personal authority is like a refreshing breeze to all who hear him.

But if his words amaze them, his actions leave them thunderstruck. An outburst from a man with an unclean spirit interrupts Jesus's teaching. The demon controlling the man sees Jesus as a threat and speaks, 'I know who you are – the Holy One of God!' (v. 24). Jesus does not have to conduct an elaborate exorcism ritual. With a word of authority he rebukes the spirit and restores the man to wholeness.

His authority is recognised – with fear by those who have everything to lose, and with amazement by those who have nothing to fear. His credentials as the Holy One of God are established.

To reflect on
Jesus passed his authority on to his disciples (16:17) and he offers it to us today.

WEDNESDAY 4 JULY
Simon's Mother-in-law

Mark 1:29–31

'Simon's mother-in-law was in bed with a fever, and they told Jesus about her' (v. 30, NIV).

As Peter rushed out the door that morning, he called over his shoulder to me, 'Oh, Mum, there'll be a few extras for lunch.' Then he was gone. 'What did he say?' I asked my daughter. She repeated it, explaining about Peter's new group of friends and the man Jesus who is causing such a stir in the area. Well, far from feeling delighted at the prospect of meeting this fellow for myself, I was annoyed. For one thing, I wish Peter would stop calling me 'Mum'. I'm not his mother and he knows my name – Lil.

And what exactly did he mean by 'a few extras'? That really steamed me up. After all, I've got to watch the budget. Who was going to pay for the extra? And, besides that, it would be terribly embarrassing if there wasn't enough to go round. I felt really hot under the collar, and then by mid-morning my head was spinning and I really did have a fever, not just one of annoyance. My daughter helped me into bed and there I lay for the rest of the morning.

I must have been asleep when Peter came in with his new friend. Jesus, a tall, thin chap with deep, calm eyes, took my hand and laid his other hand on my forehead. He smiled at me and said something quietly, and all of a sudden the world stopped spinning. It went, just like that, the fever and the annoyed feelings. I felt a real calm inside me as I prepared a meal for them – six or eight, I think, I didn't really count. But the reheated casserole that usually feeds only the three of us went round twice, and those fisherman fellows are all big eaters. Peter caught my eye at one stage and said, 'Thanks, Lil, you're a great mum.' I found myself smiling back at him. 'You're welcome, son,' I said. 'There'll be fish pie for lunch tomorrow if you want to bring your friends back.'

To reflect on
Simon's mother-in-law – was she transformed, or merely healed?

THURSDAY 5 JULY
The Beginning of the Crowds

Mark 1:32–34

'The whole town gathered at the door, and Jesus healed many who had various diseases' (vv. 33–34, NIV).

In one action-packed Sabbath, Jesus's days of anonymity are over. Early to the synagogue for the service at which he spoke; a dramatic dealing with the man with the unclean spirit; coming back to Peter's house for lunch, only to find Peter's mother-in-law sick and needing his healing touch; and now at sunset, a crowd of people craving his attention. Along with them another crowd, 'the whole city', who had come to 'rubberneck' and watch the action.

Coming to Jesus at this time of day was more than avoiding the heat of the day. The Sabbath, the day of rest, lasted from sunset on Friday to sunset on Saturday. The Jewish leaders had proclaimed that it was against the law to be healed on the Sabbath (*Matt 12:10; Luke 13:14*). Another law prohibited travelling on the Sabbath, and yet another forbade the carrying of any burden through a town on the Sabbath (*cf. Jer 17:21,22*) as that would have been work, and work was forbidden. So the sick people and those who brought them waited until sunset before coming for their healing.

The people came because they had heard about Jesus and knew he could do what was needed to heal and restore them. It is a picture of confidence and trust in his ability to show forth the power of God. But there is also sadness in this same scene as the people came, not out of love for him, nor in order to sign up as his followers, but to get what they could.

The demons knew him, but he silenced them. Jesus's mission was not to provide fresh sensations for the six o'clock news. He was not after personal glory or publicity. While the miracles were 'news value' and certainly good news for those who received from him, they were not the sum total of *the* good news, which would also involve suffering and death. A demonic testimony would not tell the whole story. At this stage the crowd could only marvel.

To reflect on
What is your motivation for following Jesus?

FRIDAY 6 JULY

Caught in the Act!

Mark 1:35–39

'Very early in the morning, while it was still dark, Jesus got up, left the house and went off to a solitary place, where he prayed' (v. 35, NIV).

After his exhausting Sabbath, we catch a glimpse of a very human Jesus getting up early, trying not to wake the others, and tiptoeing out of the house to find a quiet and isolated spot where he could pray. For him, there was no lie-in after a busy Sunday, with breakfast TV, muesli and black coffee, and a leisurely look at the morning paper!

If prayer was so important to Jesus, the Son of God, how much more must it be vital – life-giving – for us. He prayed in the early hours of the morning, away from people, before the endless demands of human need hit him.

Jesus' need for secluded prayer makes it clear that his authority, strength and power come from God alone (see 9:29). But Simon and his companions 'hunt him down'. The strong word used here suggests that it has been an urgent manhunt to find him. They interrupt his moments of private prayer to inform him that everyone in Capernaum is looking for him, and urge him to return to the scene of the previous day's triumphs and glory.

This episode is the first hint that the disciples will create more trouble for Jesus than support. They are looking for him in Capernaum because of the miracles, not because of his words, and the disciples would like to make the most of this surge in popularity. Jesus is not interested in the passing favour of the crowds and refuses to go back to Capernaum. His calling is to preach to all Israel.

The good news is never static. It never rests on yesterday's victory laurels. Throughout Mark's Gospel, Jesus is always on the move, taking with him those who can keep the pace. He is a man on a mission and will not be distracted from his divine purpose, even by success and glory. Mark tells us (v. 39) that it is no longer rumours that are flying about Galilee (v. 28) but Jesus himself.

Prayer
Lord, for yesterday I thank you,
for today I say 'yes',
for tomorrow I trust you.

SATURDAY 7 JULY

Untouchable

Mark 1:40–45

'A man with leprosy came to him and begged him on his knees, "If you are willing, you can make me clean" ' (v. 40, NIV).

There is one in every school. It's the person who spends every break by himself in the corner of the playground, or asks the teacher if it's possible to stay inside and help rather than go outside. He may have an accent that is different from everyone else's, or a funny smell, or a strange way of doing things.

There is one in every workplace. It's the person who hasn't found a way of mixing with the rest of the staff. She may eat lunch by herself because she is too shy to seek company, or so loud that people joke about her behind her back. She may have a body that is too big, or too small, or different from what is thought of as normal.

There is one in every church. It's the person who has never quite fitted in with the rest of the congregation. She may wear clothes that look poor in a rich area, or clothes that look rich in a poor area. She might be ill, or awkward, or needy. She might have green hair, a pierced tongue, a baby but no husband.

Do you know any 'outcasts' like that?

Mark tells us of an outcast who was not only physically repugnant, but socially and religiously undesirable. Those suffering with leprosy were the equivalent of Hindu 'untouchables', viewed as non-persons and treated as if they were the living dead.

Notice the way Jesus responds to him. The man was covered with leprosy, but his desperation did not make him forget himself. As he came to Jesus he knelt down, humbling himself. Jesus felt so deeply for the man that he was moved to action. He touched him – unthinkable! The man was healed – unbelievable! Jesus told him to go and be examined by the priest – understandable! And to remain silent – impossible!

To reflect on
An AIDS sufferer said, 'Sometimes I have a terrible feeling that I am dying not from the virus, but from being untouchable.'

SUNDAY 8 JULY
The Prayer of a Person Falsely Accused

Psalm 7

'My shield is God Most High, who saves the upright in heart'
(v. 10, NIV).

'You said...!' 'I did not!' 'You did so!' It's like a childish spat, usually harmless, and familiar to most parents! 'Get it sorted' seems to be the modern response.

For David, the 'spat' was far more serious. It is thought that he wrote Psalm 7 in response to the slanderous accusations of those who claimed he was trying to kill King Saul and seize the throne (1 Sam 24:9–11). Instead of striking back, David cried out to God for justice. He looked for refuge, not revenge.

His words are graphic and colourful. He is pursued by enemies who are out to get him, not with swords but with words, a more powerful weapon. Their false accusations are like the sharp teeth of a ravaging lion, and in desperation he cries out to God. He swears his innocence of the charges laid against him. If indeed he had done certain things, then his enemies would have every right to pursue him, and God would have every right to punish him.

But he knows he is innocent and so he cries, 'Arise... rise up... awake... decree.' The urgency is not to waken a sleeping God, but while the false accusations remain unanswered, they suggest that God is powerless and the slanderers victorious. In a powerful metaphor of conception, pregnancy and birth, he depicts the evil they are hatching. He pleads his own righteousness and integrity as proof of his innocence and casts himself upon God.

In the final verse of the psalm, he vows to praise. As need leads to prayer, so deliverance leads to praise, and thus he honours God. We are not told whether the psalmist was vindicated and his name cleared. There is no 'happy-ever-after' postscript to the psalm. We know only that having brought the matter to God in prayer, he was given strength to leave it there. His prayer-psalm is a pattern for all who are falsely accused.

'The name of the LORD is a strong tower; the righteous run to it and are safe' (Prov 18:10).

MONDAY 9 JULY
Who Is This Man?

Mark 2:1–12

'So many gathered that there was no room left, not even outside the door, and he preached the word to them' (v. 2, NIV).

I was so pleased when I heard that Jesus was coming back to Capernaum. We'd heard amazing things about him. But just who was he? My neighbour was full of it. 'They say evil spirits flee at the sound of his voice. Who do you think he is?' 'Don't ask me,' I replied, 'but I'm going to invite him here for a chat.'

I was just serving drinks when my neighbour arrived, with his whole family, and a few friends he'd invited. 'Come in,' I tried to smile, 'you're all welcome.' And come in they did. I don't know where all those people came from. Before I knew it, the place was packed. They were hanging through the windows, peering through the doors and – what was that? Something landed on my head. I looked up and, you wouldn't believe it, they were coming through the ceiling as well!

The next minute down through the ceiling came a mat, lowered to the ground, right in front of Jesus. I looked at the man lying on the mat – paralysed he was, but grinning from ear to ear. Then I heard Jesus say, 'My dear friend, your sins are forgiven.' At that, there was a gasp. Even I know that only God can forgive sins. Who is this man? Whoever he is, he seemed to know what people were thinking and asked, 'Well, which is easier? To give this man what he needs – the lifting of his guilt – or to give him what he wants – the movement of his legs?'

An uneasy silence filled the room. Then Jesus turned to the paralysed man and said, 'Get up, pick up your mat and off you go!' And he got up! And he picked up his mat! And he went! You should have heard the cheering! My neighbour nudged me. 'Wow,' he shouted, 'I reckon he's the Holy One.'

'Holy One?' I said. 'I'll show you holey one! Just you look at my roof!' 'No', he replied, 'Holy One of God. That's who I think he is. What do you think?'

TUESDAY 10 JULY
The Call of Matthew

Mark 2:13–14

'As he walked along, he saw Levi son of Alphaeus sitting at the tax collector's booth' (v. 14, NIV).

Steadily the doors of the synagogue close on Jesus, forcing him out. The open air by the lake is his arena now, a hillside or fishing boat his pulpit. The Son of God is being banned from the house of God. So he does what any rabbi would do – teaches his disciples as he walks from one place to another.

Capernaum, a major town in Galilee, was a key military centre for Roman troops as well as a thriving business community. In this strategic spot Levi (also called Matthew), a Jew, worked for Herod Antipas, collecting taxes both from citizens and from merchants passing through. Tax-collectors were hated by the Jews because of their reputation for cheating and for being in the employ of Rome.

Into this unlikely recruitment scene walks Jesus, who calls Matthew ('gift of the Lord') to follow him. More than any other disciple, Matthew would know how much it would cost to follow Jesus. When he left his tax-collecting booth, he guaranteed himself unemployment. Some of the other disciples could go back fishing if things didn't work out, but for Matthew there was no turning back. Even so, he did not hesitate.

Following Jesus, Matthew received two things – a new life and a new task. First, in accepting the call to be a follower, he himself became an accepted person. For this man it was certain that 'the old has gone, the new has come!' (2 Cor 5:17). For a man who had spent years being hated, that change must have been tremendous. Second, he was given a new purpose for his skills. He had been a record keeper and a keen observer. Responding to Jesus' call, he took his pen with him and used those skills to record the greatest story ever lived. He lost one job, but gained a far greater one. The Gospel that bears his name is his testimony.

To reflect on
Even before we respond to God's call, he is investing skills and abilities in us. Do you know that you are God's 'work of art' in progress?

WEDNESDAY 11 JULY
What a Party!

Mark 2:15–17

'While Jesus was having dinner at Levi's house, many tax collectors and "sinners" were eating with him' (v. 15, NIV).

Tony Campolo tells of being in a strange city, and going into an all-night diner. He overhears a group of prostitutes talking, one of them saying that the next day will be her birthday. One of her friends retorts, 'What do you want, a birthday party?' The first responds, 'I've never had one in my whole life, so why should I have one now?' Campolo conspires with the owner of the diner to throw a surprise party for her the next night. A cake is baked and everything prepared.

The next night, she is amazed that anyone would go to such trouble for her. She asks if she can take the cake home, but before she leaves Campolo offers to pray with her. He asks God to bless her and prays for her salvation. Hearing his prayer, the owner of the diner reacts, 'You never told me you were a preacher. What kind of church do you belong to?' Campolo responds that he belongs to a church that throws birthday parties for prostitutes at three thirty in the morning![5]

That's the same spirit as this party held at Matthew's house. The place was fair rocking with tax-collectors and 'sinners'. Some scribes who were Pharisees were there as well, observing the 'scene of scum'. These were the people who sincerely believed that religion consisted in keeping oneself holy, separated from anything or anyone that could defile. They had rules about what could be eaten, which vessels could be used, and with whom one could eat.

Jesus, in contrast, saw sinners as people to be reclaimed. By eating with them, he befriended them, bringing healing to the sick and welcome to those who were outcast. For Jesus, holiness was the power of God which could turn tax collectors into disciples. Instead of classifying people as holy or unholy, clean or unclean, righteous or sinner, Jesus gathered them all in the embrace of God's love.

To reflect on
Rules or relationships – which are more important to your faith?

THURSDAY 12 JULY
Let the Party Continue

Mark 2:18–20

'How can the guests of the bridegroom fast while he is with them?'
(v. 19, NIV).

Raise the matter of fasting at a dinner party these days and you're likely to get a cool reaction. For many in Jesus' day, however, fasting was a regular practice. Strict Jews fasted on Mondays and Thursdays from 6 a.m. to 6 p.m., after which time normal food could be eaten. The Law laid down only one annual fast, the Day of Atonement (*Lev 16:29–31*), when the whole nation was to confess their sins. By the time of the exile in the sixth century BC, four annual fasts had been added (*Zech 8:19*). People fasted when they had big decisions to make, sins to repent of, griefs to deal with or troubles to overcome.

John the Baptist's message of repentance and preparation for the one who was coming meant that fasting was appropriate for his followers. Jesus's disciples did not need to fast to prepare for his coming because he was already with them. He did not condemn fasting, but emphasised that fasting should be done with the right motives. The Pharisees would often whiten their faces when fasting, to show how devoted and holy they were.

Jesus used a vivid picture to explain to the Pharisees why his disciples did not fast. After a Jewish wedding the couple would stay at home where, for about a week, there would be feasting and rejoicing with their friends and guests. During that time of celebration, those in attendance were exempt from all religious observances, including fasting.

Jesus likened himself to the bridegroom and his followers to the chosen guests at the wedding feast. In his presence there was joy and celebration. But even as he spoke, the clouds were gathering. Jesus knew that the day was coming when he would be taken from them. The cross was already in view.

To reflect on
When my husband and I were preparing to be Salvation Army officers, our training principal was a man who fasted once a week. He said he wanted 'to let the body know who's boss'. Is fasting a discipline that would be helpful to you, for a similar reason?

FRIDAY 13 JULY
Elastic Minds Needed!

Mark 2:21–22

'No one sews a patch of unshrunk cloth on an old garment . . .
And no-one pours new wine into old wineskins' (vv. 21,22, NIV).

Jesus was an expert in taking simple, everyday, familiar objects and using them as illustrations of the kingdom. In these verses he speaks first of the danger of sewing a new patch on an old garment. The word used suggests that the new patch is made from 'undressed', that is, unwashed cloth that has not been pre-shrunk. When the garment gets wet in the rain, the new patch will shrink and tear the weaker fabric of the rest of the garment.

Second, he speaks of wine and wineskins. Before the days of bottles, a wine container was a goatskin sewn together at the edges to form a watertight bag. Fresh grape juice, giving off gases as it ferments, would expand and stretch the fresh new wineskin. But if the new wine was put into a used wineskin that had lost its elasticity and become hard and unyielding, the taut skin would burst and the wine would be wasted.

The point is clear. The Pharisees, breathing down Jesus's neck with their complex system of religious rules and regulations, had become rigid like old wineskins. The new wine that Jesus brought would be wasted if poured into such receptacles. Recent incidents had shown that the Pharisees' way of dealing with sinners was to condemn and exclude them and keep them distant. Jesus's way was to welcome and embrace them and to set them free.

Into a worn religious system, Jesus was bringing a radical, innovative, dynamic expression of a God who delights to do new things. He had come, not simply to patch up or reform the old, but to transform it. Any structures or traditions that would not bend to this new, colourful, challenging, contemporary movement would have to go.

Do you feel a personal comfort zone being extended today as you consider Jesus's words?

To reflect on
The good news of Jesus is like young wine – full of life, sparkling colour and glorious taste. Drink deeply from him today.

SATURDAY 14 JULY
Lord of the Sabbath

Mark 2:23–28

'He said to them, "The Sabbath was made for man, not man for the Sabbath" ' (v. 27, NIV).

It seems that everywhere he went, Jesus had not only his followers with him but the religious police as well. Determined to get him, they kept a critical eye on everything he and his company did.

Walking through the cornfields was not trespassing, nor was it stealing to pick the grain. The Law, set out in Lev 19:9,10 and Deut 23:25, instructed farmers to leave the corners and edges of their fields unharvested so that some of the crop could be picked by travellers and by the poor. It had to be by hand though, and not using a sickle.

But this event happened on the Sabbath, and that made all the difference. The Sabbath was tied up with thousands of rules and regulations. All work such as harvesting, reaping, winnowing, threshing and preparing a meal was forbidden. In one action the disciples broke all these rules and, in the eyes of the Pharisees, they were therefore law-breakers.

Calmly, Jesus answers them in their own language. He reminds them of the story from 1 Samuel 21:1–6, in which David was fleeing for his life and came to the tabernacle in Nob. Hungry, he demanded food, but the only food available was the holy consecrated bread. Every week twelve loaves of this bread were placed on a golden table in front of the Holy of Holies as an offering to God. At the end of the week it was replaced with fresh bread and could then be eaten by the priests, but by no one else (*Lev 24:9*). In his time of need and hunger David took the bread, gave some to his companions, and they ate it.

Quoting this incident, Jesus showed that Scripture itself contains an example of human need taking precedence over rules. The Sabbath, he said, was made for man, not man for the Sabbath.

To reflect on
In these days we are still invited to see Sunday as a gift, a day of rest in which we are called aside to worship and celebrate the resurrection of Jesus, the foundation of our faith.

SUNDAY 15 JULY
A Psalm of Creation

Psalm 8

'O LORD, our Lord, how majestic is your name in all the earth!'
(v. 9, NIV)

I had a Bible teacher once whose favourite phrase was 'We are in the presence of a great mystery!' It annoyed me then, as I looked for answers to tie everything up. The more I think about that man now, and his catch-phrase, the more I suspect he was correct. We do live in the presence of a great mystery, with unanswerable questions that refuse to be neatly shelved.

David knew that he lived daily in the presence of mystery and wonder. Maybe those nights he spent as a shepherd boy out on the hillsides or in the desert, with only sheep and stars to keep him company, opened his heart to wonder. However it happened, he had caught a glimpse of the majesty and might of God, and of his own insignificance.

Our reaction is similar, whether it is something microscopically small that we observe – such as the fine bones in a human ear, the activity of a colony of ants, the lights of glow-worms in a dark cave – or something macroscopically huge, like a view of the Grand Canyon, a Swiss mountain in snowy cover, or the canopy of stars on a clear Zambian night. These sights remind us that we live in the presence of many things greater than ourselves.

Observing the majesty of God's creation, David cried out, 'In view of all this greatness, how is it that you also think of me?' In response, God showed him that mankind has been placed at the centre of the world, second only to heavenly beings, and has been given mastery and dominion over all creatures of the earth.

We often trudge through life, heads down, kicking our feet through grey puddles, overwhelmed by needs and burdens that have taken centre stage. Today, Psalm 8 invites you to lift your head and to let both small and huge things remind you that God is aware of you, knows you, loves you. You are a significant part of the limitless universe he has created.

Today let your 'now' become 'wow!'

MONDAY 16 JULY
Spot the Sabbath-Breakers!

Mark 3:1–6

'Some of them were looking for a reason to accuse Jesus, so they watched him closely to see if he would heal him on the Sabbath' (v. 2, NIV).

Jesus' return to the synagogue inevitably caused a showdown. The Pharisees were there, their motive clearly identifying them. They had come, not to point people to God, which was their task as religious leaders, but to find reasons to accuse Jesus. They were envious of his popularity, annoyed by his miracles, shaken by the authority with which he spoke. And so they sat, front row, in the seats of honour.

Also present that day was a man with a withered hand. It was not a birth defect but the result of an illness or accident, and obviously not life-threatening. That was the point. If the man's complaint had been life-threatening, then Jesus would have every right to deal with it, for the Law allowed such mercy. But if not, then the man could come back tomorrow, because to heal on the Sabbath was work, and that was forbidden. The Pharisees had no doubt that Jesus could heal the man. The question was, 'would he?'

Jesus called him to the front, to stand where everyone could see him. Making his point crystal clear, Jesus turned to the Pharisees and asked them two questions. 'Is it lawful to do good or to do evil on the Sabbath?' If they were to give any answer, it would be to admit that it was lawful to do good and that it was unlawful to do evil.

With no answer forthcoming, he asked two more questions. 'Is it lawful to save life or to kill on the Sabbath?' Here was Jesus, ready to heal, and here were they, ready to murder. No wonder they had nothing to say! Angry at their hardness of heart, Jesus spoke a word of power and the man's hand was restored.

'Immediately' – still on the Sabbath – the Pharisees went out and conspired with the Herodians (unclean Romans with whom they would have had nothing to do previously) how to get rid of Jesus. A man's withered hand is eclipsed by this display of withered souls.

To reflect on
This incident is all about rules versus mercy. Which characterises your faith?

TUESDAY 17 JULY
The Rising Tide of Popularity

Mark 3:7–12

'Whenever the evil spirits saw him, they fell down before him and cried out, "You are the Son of God" ' (v. 11, NIV).

Jesus's withdrawal from the synagogue is not an admission of fear or defeat, but simply that his hour has not yet come. Back to the open air and the lakeside, he finds the crowds flocking to him. The crowds come not only from the area around Capernaum, but also from distant parts of Israel and its surrounding neighbours.

Jesus can withdraw from those who are conspiring against him (3:6), but he cannot escape the demanding crowds. The exuberant crush of people stands in stark contrast to the grim faces of the teachers of the Law. Some come out of curiosity, others come for healing. Some come hunting for evidence to use against him, while others, sincere seekers, come wanting to know if he truly is the Messiah. Most of them can scarcely begin to understand the real significance of his presence among them. Mark believed that they were more interested in 'all he was doing' than what he said (v. 8). The crowds are so large and the sick people so insistent and anxious for his healing touch that he asks for a boat to be kept ready for him, just off shore, from where he can speak at a safe distance. How human this Jesus is!

The crowds 'fall upon him', but the demons 'fall before him' and blurt out his identity. But Jesus continues to prevent them from making him known. His rebuke of the demons shows his power over them in the same way that he rebukes the wind and tells the sea to be still (4:39). He both expels and silences them with a word.

But he has another reason for silencing them. The ravings of demons will never reveal the whole truth. Jesus wanted to have time to teach people about the kind of Messiah he really was – far different from their expectations. The people thought of Messiahship in terms of Jewish nationalism. He thought of Messiahship in terms of love.

To reflect on
Jesus's kingdom is spiritual. It begins not with the overthrow of governments, but with the overthrow of sin in people's hearts.

WEDNESDAY 18 JULY
Pick Me! Pick Me!

Mark 3:13–19a

'He appointed twelve – designating them apostles – that they might be with him and that he might send them out to preach and to have authority to drive out demons' (vv. 14,15, NIV).

When Jesus chose his team, he didn't first line up all the hopefuls and then pick according to strength or obvious superiority. The team he did choose was a rather motley lot. There were a few fine ones, like Andrew and Bartholomew, but then there were:

- Simon Peter ('Rocky') – more rock-headed, at times, than solid and dependable.
- James and John ('Sons of Thunder') – did that mean they were judgmental and argumentative, exploding all over the place, such as when they called down fire on a Samaritan village?
- Simon the Zealot – a fiery, violent nationalist, a freedom fighter who was committed to clearing the country of the hated Romans.
- Matthew, the tax-collector – in the employ of those same hated Romans. Put these last two in a dark alley together, and only one would emerge!
- And then there was Judas. Didn't Jesus know the choices this man would eventually make?

What was it that Jesus saw in this ragtag lot? It seems easier to answer that question with a list of 'nots'. Not their faith, not their talent, not their obvious ability. But he must have seen in them a willingness to obey and to throw their whole hearts into following him.

Notice that he called them first to be with him. That meant more than just hanging around with him. Being with him meant allowing his message to be written on their hearts, following wherever he led, sharing the toil of ministry, the harassment of the crowds (see 3:20). Would they have signed up if Gethsemane had been advertised in advance?

Second, he called them to send them out. They would be not just receptors, but channels of his healing power. Jesus still says, 'Come, learn from me, then go and tell.'

To reflect on

If God made up his team just with the strong and gifted, then I wouldn't qualify, and you probably wouldn't either. God's team is still open for anyone who is whole-hearted and willing to obey his call.

THURSDAY 19 JULY
A Sad Family

Mark 3:20–21

'When his family heard about this, they went to take charge of him, for they said, "He is out of his mind" ' (v. 21, NIV).

These few verses offer us a sad glimpse into a very human family trying, but failing, to understand a divine son. His mother and brothers come to take him away. The account is interrupted at v. 22 and then picked up again in v. 31. They come to round him up, not to rally around him. As we stand with that huddled family group, can we enter into what they must have been feeling?

Jesus had grown up in the family home in Nazareth, working in the carpenter's shop which, tradition says, Joseph had left to him. Then suddenly it seems, he had thrown it all in and gone off to be a wandering preacher. Had he explained his mission before he left? To add to the family's anxiety, reports of Jesus's regular clashes with the orthodox religious leaders were no doubt reaching their ears. They would know the power of these people, and the foolishness of tackling them.

What was more, he had gathered a band of people around him, a strange group at that – some fishermen, a reformed tax-collector, a fanatical nationalist. What sort of influence would these friends have on him? Where would they lead him? Such questions would come naturally to a concerned mother.

They had seen this loved son and brother throw away all that stood for security, and now here he was, not even seeming to care about what people were saying. He was taking risks that, in their opinion, no man in his right mind would take. But there was a final straw. 'Again a crowd gathered, so that he and his disciples were not even able to eat' (v. 20). Any mother would be anxious about such neglect of necessities!

And so they came to remove him. Their action was prompted by concern and a desire to protect him from danger. How tragic that those who were closest to Jesus were so slow to understand who he was and what he came to do.

To reflect on
How well do I understand the motivation of those who are closest to me?

FRIDAY 20 JULY
A Smear Campaign

Mark 3:22–30

'The teachers of the law who came down from Jerusalem said, "He is possessed by Beelzebub!" ' (v. 22, NIV).

The crowds flock to hear him (3:8); his family come to silence him (3:21); the scribes come to defame him (3:22). These theological specialists cannot deny Jesus' miracles and supernatural power. The evidence is all around them. But to admit that his power is from God will leave them no choice but to accept him as the Messiah. In an attempt to halt his surging popularity, they launch a smear campaign, accusing him of having power from Satan. They have no more understanding of his mission than his family do.

In response to their accusation that he is possessed by Beelzebub, 'the prince of demons', Jesus speaks to them in parables which draw out the absurdity of their claim. If their charge is correct, then Satan is irrationally trying to do himself in. But if Jesus is not an agent of the devil, then the explanation must be that a stronger man has bound Satan and is ransacking his house. What is happening is not the result of civil war within Satan's ranks, but a direct onslaught from outside.

In this parable the strong one is Satan. His house is his domain, the present world, which he seeks to hold secure. His possessions are the victims he has taken captive. The stronger one is Jesus, who has come from God, crushed Satan's stronghold and overcome and bound him. Jesus's healing and deliverance miracles are evidence of his power to set free those who have been in Satan's clutches.

Rejecting Jesus out of ignorance is one thing, but attacking the power by which he works is something far more serious. The sworn enemies of Jesus have shut their eyes and their hearts to the truth in a deliberate act of blindness. Their sin is unforgivable.

This incident is a defining moment for Jesus. He will no longer attempt to coax these hard-hearted, murder-plotting leaders to faith. Rather, he will invest his energies in sowing seeds of faith in the hearts of those who are sincerely willing to follow him.

To reflect on
The lines are drawn – where do you stand?

SATURDAY 21 JULY
Redefining the Family

Mark 3:31–35

'Here are my mother and my brothers! Whoever does God's will is my brother and sister and mother' (vv. 34,35, NIV).

When my grandson David was almost three years old he became aware of the large extended family that surrounds him, and was fascinated to work out just who belongs to whom. It was quite a discovery when he realised that I am not only his Granbar, but also his daddy's mummy and Grandad's lady!

One day as we sat looking at the trees blowing in the wind and talking about God who made them, he asked me with wide eyes, 'What's God's lady's name called?' I thought – and prayed – very quickly, and then replied, 'Well, God has lots of ladies. I'm one of God's ladies, and so is your Mummy, and so is Nan.' He seemed content with that answer, but it set me thinking.

From the moment of our birth until the time we die, we are defined by who we belong to. A birth notice announces that a child is born 'to Jim and Joan'. An engagement notice proclaims that 'Mary, daughter of Harry and Brenda, is going to marry Alistair, son of Rex and Pam'. A death notice says that 'Lee, beloved spouse of Sam' has died. When being introduced it is often as a daughter/son/sister/parent of someone. Our family relationships tell us where we have come from, who we belong to and who we are.

When Jesus's family came looking for him, he redefined what it means to belong to his family. His response was an embrace of all who enter God's family by an act of faith and trust (see John 1:12,13) and then live in allegiance to God's purposes. The only membership requirements in this new Messianic family are obeying God and following what Jesus taught and did.

May the invitation to be a member of God's family fill your heart with wonder today. May this word give you courage to reach out to someone else who may not be part of your biological family, but who is your brother or sister because of the relationship you share in Christ.

Prayer
Bind us together, Lord, bind us together with love.

SUNDAY 22 JULY

In Praise of God's Name

Psalm 9

'I will be glad and rejoice in you; I will sing praise to your name,
O Most High' (v. 2, NIV).

Psalm 9 is a song of praise for God's deliverance. The psalmist begins by expressing his intention. 'I will praise you ... I will tell ... I will be glad ... I will sing praise to your name.' What a wonderful pattern for testimony these verses contain – the public recounting of God's work, the experience of rejoicing and exultation, and the singing of praise concerning God's name. Such praise comes from the heart and embraces the whole being. Compare David's words elsewhere, 'Praise the Lord, O my soul; all my inmost being, praise his holy name' (Ps 103:1).

God is praised for his wonderful works (v. 1) and for his name (vv. 2,10). What he has done tells us who he is! The name of the Lord, so powerfully praised in this psalm, is mentioned time and time again throughout the book of Psalms. To pray is to call upon his name (Ps 80:18). His name protects (Ps 20:1). His name saves (Ps 54:1). His name brings confidence and hope (Ps 52:9). His name is to be trusted (Ps 20:7). His name brings joy (Ps 89:16). His name is a place of refuge and security (Ps 69:36). Those who know his name are those who know his character and nature, and who choose to live in obedience to his will. To these God says, 'Because he loves me, I will rescue him; I will protect him, for he acknowledges my name' (Ps 91:14).

In contrast to God, whose name and reign have been established for ever (v. 7), the name of the wicked will one day be forgotten, blotted out for ever, so that no memory of their existence will remain. To the Jewish people, such a fate would be unspeakable.

While God stands centre stage in this psalm, his enemies lurk somewhere in the wings. The psalmist knows the final victory has not yet been won, but he is confident. God's powerful victories in the past give assurance that he is still in charge for the future.

Today, find a way to express your praise to the name of God.

PROVERBS IN PERSON

Introduction

I was in my early teen years when black-and-white television came to New Zealand and we bought our first set. I had no idea how it worked, but my mother would say, 'In the morning we will have to clean up all the dead bodies of the cowboys and Indians lying behind the set.'

When I read the book of Proverbs with its colourful word pictures, I get the impression that there are real people lurking behind these verses. For example:

- 'A gossip betrays a confidence, but a trustworthy man keeps a secret' (11:13)
- 'A wife of noble character is her husband's crown, but a disgraceful wife is like decay in his bones' (12:4)
- 'The way of the sluggard is blocked with thorns, but the path of the upright is a highway' (15:19)
- 'A man of many companions may come to ruin, but there is a friend who sticks closer than a brother' (18:24)
- 'A corrupt witness mocks at justice, and the mouth of the wicked gulps down evil' (19:28)
- 'Discipline your son, and he will give you peace; he will bring delight to your soul' (29:17)

Many of the word pictures of Proverbs remind me of actual people whom I know. Here is a selection of some of them. As you read these real-life cameos of 'Proverbs in Person', maybe you too will recognise some people you know, walking around in this colourful part of the Bible. You might even come across a verse that describes you, yourself! Happy hunting!

MONDAY 23 JULY
A Man Who Is Skilled in his Work

Proverbs 22:17–29

'Do you see a man skilled in his work? He will serve before kings; he will not serve before obscure men' (v. 29, NIV)

I know a man who makes this verse from Proverbs come alive. You wouldn't notice him in a crowd. He is slight of stature, dresses modestly, walks with quiet tread. There's nothing about him that makes him stand out, nothing loud or garish or conspicuous.

Discipline and integrity mark his path. He has a fine mind which he has developed through years of reading and study. He is most at home in a museum or a library. Watch him handle a book, and it is an action of deep respect, almost worship, as he honours the author's work, admires the feel of the binding and draws in the fragrance of the pages. He's an ordered, tidy man. Doing dishes becomes a work of art as he rinses and stacks the pile and then proceeds in orderly fashion.

Doing dishes, the background task, supporting others, these would be his chosen arena of service. When I needed help with words, he was there. When I was hunting out background information, he knew exactly where to look. When it comes to reading maps and timetables, he's an expert. In his service for God this man has shunned the public limelight, but delights in being behind the scenes, making things easier for others. He would have been content to be overlooked, passed by in favour of someone else.

But those with eyes to see in fact saw some of the gems in this man, and have set him in a high place. He's still serving with a humble spirit, still resourcing others and doing the ordered task, but these days, it's before kings that he stands.

To reflect on
Could this verse be a description of you?

TUESDAY 24 JULY
An Offended Sister

Proverbs 18:15–24

'An offended brother [– or sister –] is more unyielding than a fortified city, and disputes are like the barred gates of a citadel'
(v. 19, NIV).

I know a woman for whom this verse from Proverbs is sadly true.

Mrs A and Mrs B were firm friends. They had known each other a long time. Their children had grown up together. Mrs A was a keen leader among the local corps women. Mrs B organised the jumble sales. They were both 'pillars of the place', respected for who they were and valued for their work.

Then something happened. No one ever really knew what caused the upset, but Mrs A and Mrs B were both suddenly 'relieved of their duties' and replaced. Mutterings behind the scenes indicated that 'it' hadn't been handled well, whatever 'it' was.

Mrs A took some time to get over the upset. She had felt a real calling to work with the women of the corps and the neighbourhood. Eventually she returned, picking up her leadership role again, deeper somehow, more compassionate and understanding of those with whom she worked.

Mrs B never got over the incident. She cut her ties with the corps and closed herself off from every attempt that others made to reach out and reconcile. She locked herself up behind barred gates of bitterness and unforgiveness, and threw away the key. She became a grey figure, living in a grey house, hiding behind grey curtains of loneliness and suspicion.

How quickly bitterness in the heart becomes a prison where the unforgiving person takes on the role of both prisoner and guard at the door. Jesus acknowledged that forgiveness is not easy, nor does it come cheaply, but he spoke of it as an essential ingredient in God's forgiveness toward us. The key to our own forgiveness, he said, is in our own hands.

To reflect on
Today, is there someone you need to forgive? Let God help you to unlock the barred gates of bitterness and make your way out into the warm sunshine of forgiveness.

WEDNESDAY 25 JULY
Hope Deferred Makes the Heart Sick

Proverbs 13:8–17

'Hope deferred makes the heart sick, but a longing fulfilled is a tree of life' (v. 12, NIV).

I know a woman who makes this verse from Proverbs come alive. To look at her, you would consider that she has everything going for her. She's tall, slim, dark-haired and attractive. She is a warm person with an appealing, pensive nature. She is well-educated, qualified in her chosen area, articulate, well travelled. Her strong creative skills are apparent in the artistic, gifted nature of her children. Her husband is like an oak tree, growing strongly beside her and giving protection to all the family. She lives in a spacious house in a safe neighbourhood and in a great country.

But for a long time, longer than she likes to recall, the inner landscape of her life has been barren and bleak. Depression settled on her heart like a heavy blanket. She became an expert in hopelessness, knowing all its ghastly nooks and crannies, recognising all its disguises. She became attuned to the voices of hopelessness, torn between giving in to their taunts and the longing not to hurt her children.

People tried to help her. A host of medical agencies made all their services available to her. Friends stood by, loving, caring, praying, trusting God for her healing. Family members grieved for her and reassured her of their commitment and love. But nothing seemed to make a difference.

Then one day, not so long ago, a tiny shaft of light penetrated her inner gloom. Like a determined flower growing up through a crack in the concrete, a fragile moment of 'maybe' caught her heart and lifted her spirit. A new diagnosis came together with new medication, a new working environment, new reassurances of love, and a fresh word from God: 'God is within her, she will not fall; God will help her at break of day' (Ps 46:5).

It's still too early for her to see trees growing lush and healthy on the inner landscape. But there are some precious buds of hope showing, enough to propel her forward into life.

To reflect on
'The light shines in the darkness, but the darkness has not overcome it' (John 1:5).

THURSDAY 26 JULY
A Man of Woe

Proverbs 33: 29–35

'Who has woe? Who has sorrow? . . . Those who linger over wine . . .' (vv. 29,30).

I know a man who had many years of woe and sorrow because he lingered long over wine.

He was a man with great practical skills, but an accident put him out of work. One day, his wife pointed out an advertisement for the job of cleaning the Salvation Army hall. He was hesitant at first. As an avowed atheist, he was somewhat cautious of Christians, but necessity demanded action so he applied for the job and got it.

He was a conscientious worker and was happy to have a cup of coffee with the corps officers when the job was done. He thought at first they looked a bit 'dodgy', but he enjoyed their long talks together. He made it quite clear to them that he had no intention of becoming a Christian.

As the years went by he drank more and more, until his marriage broke up and he left the family home. One day, a friend gave him a video on the life of Jesus and, as he watched it, a miracle happened. This man, who had often declared that there was nothing in religion for him, was soundly converted!

He made inquiries as to the whereabouts of those former corps officers and rang them. 'Remember me?' he asked, 'I'm that hopeless case you used to make coffee for! I've just become a Christian. It happened eleven hours ago, but really it started way back in those days when I cleaned the hall, and you guys listened to my ramblings!'

He spent the next few years 'drying out' and learning to live a Christian life. The hardest part for him these days is not alcohol, but twenty years of life that have been erased from his memory. He cannot recall his children as babies or toddlers, and has only vague memories of where he has been and who he has worked for.

But one thing he does remember is that the Lord's compassions never fail. 'They are new every morning; great is [his] faithfulness' (*Lam 3:22,23*).

FRIDAY 27 JULY
A Cheerful Heart

Proverbs 17:22–28

'A cheerful heart is good medicine' (v. 22, NIV).

I know two women who make this proverb come alive. One is in her mid-nineties, the other in her youthful mid-eighties. They have been friends for about seventy years, having first met when H. was a young Salvation Army captain and T. still a schoolgirl.

Their lives took similar paths, into Salvation Army officership, nursing training, the matronship of a series of Bethany maternity hospitals, and senior appointments in social work and administration. When H. retired she cared for her mother until she went to heaven at the age of 100. Then, on T.'s retirement, they set up home together. H. quipped at that time that she was seventy-two years old before she could go flatting with her girlfriend!

For the past twenty-plus years, they have cared for each other, maintained a wide and active interest in their beloved Army and opened their home in loving hospitality. These days they are grateful for those who come in to help with the housework and the preparation of meals. Eyesight is failing for both, but a reading machine helps them to decipher letters. H. is unsteady on her feet and her hearing is not good. But in spite of all the limitations, love and laughter fill the home. They are the kind of people whom one visits, and comes away feeling much better for having visited!

At a celebration recently for her ninety-fifth birthday, H. stood to give her speech. Thanking everyone for coming, she said, 'I feel as if I am standing on the shore of a vast ocean of love, and all I need is a surfboard!'

These two friends live each day within glimpsing distance of heaven. Their physical limitations mean that much of the detail of life passes them by. But every day with cheerful, grateful hearts they drink deeply from the love of God, testifying that he is still their song of joy and their salvation.

To reflect on
'Laughter is the sun that drives the winter from the human face.'
(Victor Hugo)

SATURDAY 28 JULY
Better a Dry Crust with Peace and Quiet

Proverbs 17:1–8

'Better a dry crust with peace and quiet than a house full of feasting, with strife' (v. 1, NIV).

I know a young couple who took hold of this verse from Proverbs and made it the motto for their relationship.

They first met during their last year of high school when he moved to the city where she had always lived. He liked her smiling eyes, her creative school projects and her passion for God. She liked his strong, quiet manner, his sense of humour and his passion for God!

As their friendship grew, they sensed that this relationship was a special gift to them both, and they needed to care for it. They made a conscious decision to give full attention to the spiritual, rather than the physical aspects of getting to know each other, and that's where the verse from Proverbs came in. They chose the restraint of a non-physical relationship and enjoyed the blessing of God in that choice.

As their school year finished they moved into further studies, but kept talking, exploring, reading, walking, praying and worshipping together. They shared their deepest secrets and dreams and talked about life plans together. They both worked hard at becoming friends with each other's parents, keeping the relationship always out in the open, where their respective families could bless and encourage them.

The kiss during the ceremony on their wedding day was their very first kiss!

In a world where the word 'chastity' has a rather old-fashioned ring to it, such a standard seems unusual, if not impossible. Chastity, for this young couple, meant waiting, with patience and with reverence for each other and for the relationship that God was giving them. Nobody creates a masterpiece, or writes a great thesis, or composes a piano concerto in one day. Achieving anything great, including a great relationship, requires patience, hard work and commitment.

Pray today for young people you know, that they will make wise and 'chaste' choices in the relationships God opens up to them.

SUNDAY 29 JULY

The Victim's Prayer

Psalm 10

'You hear, O LORD, the desire of the afflicted; you encourage them, and you listen to their cry' (v. 17, NIV).

Newspapers are full of them. Reports of murders and muggings, slanders and slayings, which give this psalm a very modern sound.

- A remote country home is invaded in the early hours of the morning. A woman is beaten and left with life-threatening injuries.
- A gang rampages through a church, smashing the altar and tearing down the banners that proclaim God's salvation.
- A loan shark sees his opportunity with a young couple who desperately need money to travel the long journey back home for a family funeral.
- A church member stands in court and swears her testimony is true, while the man in the dock hangs his head, knowing that what is being said is all lies.
- An elderly couple invest their life savings in a trust for their children, not knowing that the lawyer who deals with them has his own schemes in mind.

Where are you, God? Where are you when people are in trouble like this, when the godly and innocent suffer at the hands of those who give no thought to you? Where are you when the wicked seem to do so well, sleek and healthy, living off the fat of the land, trampling on others in their stampede to the top? Why do you hide yourself when your children need you to intervene and act on their behalf? The psalmist gives graphic examples from his day of the innocent suffering and the wicked smirking.

His psalm starts with a 'why' of complaint, but ends with a cry of confidence. 'The victim commits himself to you; you are the helper of the fatherless' (v. 14), that is, anyone who lacks protection. Sometimes, there is no answer to the 'why' questions. Yet there is always a place of pleading before the Lord who is King for ever and ever (v. 16), a God who hears (v. 17), and who will act (v. 18). For anyone who is a victim, there is a place of refuge and protection.

Pray today for someone you know who is suffering and who needs God's help.

CALLED TO BE THE PEOPLE OF GOD
Introduction

A journey through the book of Exodus has been called 'a trip across holy ground'. This is a story of history, clothed in faith. God's people, once highly favoured in the land, are now slaves. Exodus records the story of their liberation and the miracles and means by which God forged a holy nation from a group of powerless, struggling, oppressed people.

It begins in gloom and ends in glory. God gives Israel his special name, his special deliverance, his special guidance, his special covenant, his special worship, his special mercy and his special description of himself.

It is a gripping story filled with colour and drama. There is rescue and response, celebration and complaining, grace and grumbling. It is a story of a God who always takes the initiative on behalf of those who do not deserve it, a God who is present with his people, a God who rescues, protects, guides, provides for, forgives and disciplines the people who call him their God, and who are called to be his people.

It is a story that is essential reading for this day and age, for it contains principles for daily living as up to date as tomorrow. God still goes before his people to lead us out of bondage – whether political, economic, social or spiritual – to the freedom of his kingdom of grace and glory.

The Tabernacle (chapters 25–31, 35–40), with its patterns for worship, will feature as a separate study in a later edition of *Words of Life*.

When Moses walked forward to take a closer look at the burning bush that strangely was not being burnt, he came into God's presence. As we come to this study of the book of Exodus, let us also take off our shoes, for this is holy ground.

MONDAY 30 JULY
Slavery in Egypt!

Exodus 1:1–22

'These are the names of the sons of Israel who went to Egypt with Jacob, each with his family' (v. 1, NIV).

'These are the names' – so begins the book of Exodus. This phrase stretches like a bridge back to Jacob and his sons in Canaan (see *Gen 46:8*) and forward to the population explosion of their descendants in Egypt. The naming of Jacob's twelve sons is a link with both the past and the future. The seventy who came to Egypt 'were fruitful', 'multiplied greatly', 'became exceedingly numerous', and 'the land was filled with them' (*v. 7*). In one verse of text, we have the picture of a teeming swarm of people, an almost unnatural family growth that could only be explained in God-terms. Surely this was what God had promised to Abraham, way back in Genesis 17.

A shadow passes over this picture of fertility and blessing, however, with the introduction of a new king 'who did not know about Joseph' (*v. 8*). This ruler, the first of new dynasty, had no obligation to respect or even inform himself of any previous commitments to a group of foreigners within his territory.

Moreover, these people were different. They worshipped one God; the Egyptians worshipped many gods. The Hebrews were shepherds and wanderers; the Egyptians were builders, with a deeply-rooted culture. The Hebrews lived in Goshen, physically out of the way, but numerically a threat.

Pharaoh thus chose his course of action. Spurred on by fear that they would organise themselves and threaten his kingdom, he made them slaves, to kill their spirit and stop their growth. But the more they were oppressed, the more they multiplied and spread. Hebrew midwives, who feared God more than they feared Pharaoh, played their part by using their skill and shrewdness to protect the endangered baby boys.

God will not back down on his promises. A new Pharaoh, feeling threatened, will not be outdone. The scene is set for a power struggle of epic proportions!

To reflect on
How practical God is, with every detail worked out!

TUESDAY 31 JULY

The Birth of Moses

Exodus 2:1–10

'She named him Moses, saying, "I drew him out of the water"'
(v. 10, NIV).

Enter Moses. He was a 'fine child' in the eyes of his mother, or 'no ordinary child' as reported in Hebrews 11:23. The fact that he was a healthy baby gave her all the more resolve to protect him from Pharaoh's edict of death by drowning, and so she hid him, as carefully as she would a treasure. When, by three months of age, he had grown too active and too noisy to be hidden at home any longer, she very cleverly decided to hide him in the one place no Egyptian would look – in the Nile itself. That was the very place where Hebrew boy-babies were supposed to be cast. In a shrewd way, Moses' mother may be said to have obeyed Pharaoh's grim command. But she did so with a papyrus-reed container, carefully waterproofed with tar and pitch. This ark (the same word used for Noah's boat) was a lovingly made means of salvation over which a careful watch was kept from a distance.

The drama of the discovery by Pharaoh's daughter was that it was unintended and dangerous. The delight of the discovery was the totally unexpected way it turned out. The climax of the discovery was the bold action of the little boy's sister who came forward, with a convenient offer to find a wet nurse, when she saw the princess's reaction to her brother's tears. Moses' mother was thus delivered from fear to being paid to nurture her own son. The child was delivered from danger to privilege.

It is ironic to note that all Pharaoh's efforts to suppress the people of Israel, in this early part of Exodus, were thwarted by women: the midwives (1:17), the Israelite mothers (1:19), Moses' mother and sister, and even Pharaoh's own daughter. His impotence to destroy the people of God is clearly exposed.

To reflect on
How wonderfully God works out his purposes, as everyone does their part!

WEDNESDAY 1 AUGUST
Egyptian Prince or Midianite Shepherd?

Exodus 3:1–15

'God said to Moses, "I AM WHO I AM"' (v. 14, NIV).

Moses grew up surrounded by all the privilege of Pharaoh's household. But did he know who he really was? Did a distant strain of his mother's lullaby, as she rocked her baby in his waterproof basket, ever penetrate the clamorous sounds of opulence? Did he see the harsh treatment being lashed out on his people, and feel their agony?

His intervention in the incident of the Egyptian beating a Hebrew seems premeditated – he glanced 'this way and that' (2:12) before killing the Egyptian and hiding his body in the sand. The following day, intervening in a fight between two Hebrews, he was challenged in his deliverer role and fled in fear. Cut off from the Egyptians, and unrecognised by his own people, did he trudge through lonely desert sands asking, 'Who am I, God?'

He came to a distant land beyond Pharaoh's control. This strange new land of Midian was yet somehow familiar, for the God of Abraham, Isaac and Jacob was worshipped there. Moses had come home to a place he had never been before. In this hospitable place he found a loving family – a wife and a son, whose name both summed up Moses' life to this moment and pointed to a better future.

In charge of his father-in-law's flock, Moses had driven the sheep well into the wilderness in search of fresh grazing when his attention was attracted by a blazing bush, remarkable for the fact that the bush was not burned up. He heard the voice of God calling his name and was told to remove his sandals, for the ground was holy.

In this climactic encounter, Moses learned the identity of the God who had prepared him for this moment. In finding God's identity, he discovered his own as well.

To reflect on
The ground of your being is holy.
Take off your shoes!
Awaken your sleeping prophet
Believe in your Moses and go...
(Macrina Wiederkehr,
Seasons of Your Heart)

THURSDAY 2 AUGUST
A Reluctant Recruit

Exodus 4:1-17

'But Moses said, "O Lord, please send someone else" ' (v. 13, NIV).

Commissioned for his task, Moses is told to return to Egypt, confront Pharaoh and bring God's people into a 'good and spacious land, flowing with milk and honey' (3:8). The harsh constraints of slavery are going to be exchanged for the wide open spaces of freedom in a promised land. God tells Moses what will happen, but warns him that, while the leaders of Israel will accept his message, the leaders of Egypt will reject it. The implications of what God is asking him to do cause Moses to react with a string of buts:

'But who am I to do this?' (3:11)
'But who am I to say has sent me?' (3:13)
'But what if they don't believe or listen to me?' (4:1)

Patiently God provides Moses with three signs of authority: the staff changed into a serpent, the hand instantly diseased and instantly healed, and the water of the Nile that will turn into blood. Each is a divinely empowered wonder. God makes his point – the real authority and hero of this call is not Moses but God. But Moses must believe God, as Israel must believe Moses. As Moses is to carry God's message to Israel, so Israel eventually will carry God's message to the world (see Exod 19:4-6).

In spite of all the assurances, Moses remains unconvinced. How human he is! He protests, 'You may be God, but I'm still the same old Moses, heavy-lipped and thick-tongued!' God replies, 'I will help you speak and will teach you what to say' (v. 12). Moses responds, 'Sorry, Lord, please send someone else.' In exasperation, God allows Aaron, his eloquent brother, to be Moses' mouthpiece. God himself will take responsibility for both the message and the messengers.

Moses must have clung tightly to his shepherd's staff as he left for Egypt to face the greatest challenge of his life. That staff was his assurance of God's presence and power.

To reflect on
How would God respond to your reluctance today?

FRIDAY 3 AUGUST
The Deliverer Returns

Exodus 4:18–31

'Let me go back to my own people in Egypt to see if any of them are still alive' (v. 18, NIV).

Moses is finally persuaded that he himself must return to Egypt to deliver God's message, and God's people. He goes firstly to Jethro, his father-in-law, to ask permission for the journey. This request shows how deeply he has identified with his Midianite family. His reference to 'my own people in Egypt' indicates the strong memory of his roots. His stated reason for going, 'to see if any of them are still alive', is a clue both to the passage of time and to the severity of the Egyptian oppression. Without hesitation, Jethro gives his blessing.

The staff which had been Moses' shepherd's crook became, at the meeting with God in the desert, the symbol of God's presence. In Egypt it will be the means of signs and wonders as Moses persuades Pharaoh to let his people go.

The strange incident in verses 24–26 has to do with the fact that Moses had not been circumcised. Zipporah seizes the flint knife and circumcises not Moses, but her son. This vicarious circumcision was adequate in God's eyes, for he 'let him alone' (v. 26).

Moses travels on and at a God-arranged place, meets his brother Aaron. Moses is now eighty years old, Aaron eighty-three (*Exod 7:7*). Had these two men met each other since Moses was bundled up as a baby in his waterproof basket, and Aaron, just a toddler, looked on? We have glimpsed Moses' development in Pharaoh's household, and in the wide spaces of Midian, but of Aaron's preparation for this moment there has been no mention. Yet he comes, eloquent, willing, an able communicator. That he is ready to meet Moses and become his brother's spokesman seems to be a further sign of God's careful attention to detail.

Hearing that God had seen their misery and was concerned for them, the leaders of the Israelites respond appropriately – 'they bowed down and worshipped' (*4:31*).

To reflect on
God sees... God hears... God knows... I worship.

SATURDAY 4 AUGUST
Death of a Dream

Exodus 5:1–23

'Ever since I went to Pharaoh to speak in your name, he has brought trouble upon this people, and you have not rescued your people at all' (v. 23, NIV).

Euphoric over the success of his presentation to the Israelite leaders, Moses now goes, full of confidence, to Pharaoh. His approach is direct and authoritative, 'This is what the Lord says'. But Pharaoh, a no-nonsense ruler, completely sure of himself, considers the command absurd and replies sarcastically, 'Who is the Lord?' He has no experience of God, no reason to pay any attention to what he says, and letting his workforce go is the furthest thought from his mind. Moses and Aaron are shattered. The dream of deliverance dies. Outclassed and overwhelmed, their tone becomes one of begging a favour from a powerful superior (v. 3).

Pharaoh accuses Moses and Aaron of distracting the people from their work. His utter disdain for their request is further emphasised by his immediate order to their supervisors. The people obviously have too much time on their hands if they can plan a religious pilgrimage; that time must be filled up with an increased workload. Straw will no longer be provided for the brick-making – they will have to collect that for themselves now, while still keeping up with their daily quotas. Forced to obey, the people 'scatter all over Egypt' to gather trashy stubble blown about by the wind (v. 12).

The demand proves impossible. The Israelite foremen, appointed as supervisors of the workers, are whipped for their failure to see the impossible command obeyed. They take their complaint to Pharaoh with a boldness similar to Moses' approach. They get a similar disdainful response – 'Lazy, that's what you are – lazy!' (v. 17).

Frustrated and demoralised, the supervisors turn on Moses and Aaron who, far from saving their people, are now accused of bringing their very lives into jeopardy. The dream of deliverance dies a double death. Moses turns to God. In his utter defeat he has nowhere else to go.

To reflect on
Who is in charge here? Pharaoh or God?

SUNDAY 5 AUGUST
The Lord Is My Refuge

Psalm 11

'For the LORD is righteous, he loves justice; upright men will see his face' (v. 7, NIV).

Like many others, this psalm opens with a cry of despair. The psalmist is in a crisis and has turned to God for protection. Even as he does this, tempting words cross his mind: 'Why don't you run, get out of here, go somewhere safe?' Whether these are the words of well-meaning friends, or merely his own inner voice of fear, the temptation is great. Enemies are all around him, taking up their weapons, getting ready to shoot. Surely to stand firm like a hero is craziness, not courage. That just makes him an easy target. If he were to run he might be safe.

This crisis makes him feel that the foundations of life and society are being torn down. If law and order were enforced, then he would have no need to fear. Surely he deserves a 'happy-ever-after' ending to his story, just like every other good-living person!

In a brief pause in the middle of this psalm he lifts his eyes from the surrounding threats to the sovereign LORD who looks down upon him. 'The Lord is in his holy temple' (v. 4), symbolises the presence of God among his people, close at hand. 'The LORD is on his heavenly throne' symbolises his greatness over all the earth, far greater than any human enemy. This 'double vision' gives the psalmist hope. God is both immanent, present with him in his crisis, and also transcendent, far greater than, and in control of, his human predicament. He will restore justice and goodness on the earth in his good time.

The resolution is that the Lord tests both the righteous and the wicked (v. 5). For the righteous, God's tests will be a refining fire which bring them forth as pure as gold. For the wicked, the same testing fire will be like the judgment fire and brimstone that rained down upon Sodom and Gomorrah. The final outcome of this, and every such battle, is as certain as God himself is righteous!

To reflect on
When you feel like running away, run to God.

MONDAY 6 AUGUST
God Is in Control

Exodus 6:28–7:7

'I have made you like God to Pharaoh, and your brother Aaron will be your prophet' (7:1, NIV).

Moses is in the depths of despair. His obedience to the call of God has only made things worse. His people are furious with him for multiplying their workload. Pharaoh's officials are threatening to kill. God, it seems, has not kept his side of the deal.

God, however, is firmly in control. He is like a stage manager who has positioned every player and is ready now to let the action begin. Moses will see that even Pharaoh is part of God's plan. God has raised him up to 'show you my power and that my name might be proclaimed in all the earth' (*Exod 9:16*). Pharaoh's present refusal to let the people go will soon be turned, by God's power, into a hand that drives them out.

At Moses' lowest point, God speaks his name once again and, with a series of strong action words, declares what he is about to do: 'I am the LORD ... I appeared ... I established ... I have heard ... I have remembered ... I will bring you out ... I will free you ... I will redeem you ... I will take you ... I will be ... I will bring you ... I will give ... I am the LORD' (6:2–8).

Moses and Aaron respond by doing 'just as the LORD commanded them' (7:6). They go back to Pharaoh, and the plagues are unleashed on the land of Egypt. God's sovereignty is such that he brings not only Moses and Aaron, but Pharaoh, the Egyptians and even the natural world into this great epic drama.

As each gloomy plague descends upon the land, the Egyptian people realise how powerless their own gods are to stop it. Hapi, the 'powerful' god of the Nile, cannot prevent the waters from turning to blood (7:20). Hathor, the cow-goddess, is helpless as cattle die in droves (9:6). Amon-Ra, the sun god, cannot stop an eerie darkness from covering the land for three full days (10:21,22). But worse is yet to come.

To reflect on
When we reach the end of ourselves, God is waiting to act!

TUESDAY 7 AUGUST
A Distinct People

Exodus 11:1–10

'Then you will know that the LORD makes a distinction between Egypt and Israel' (v. 7, NIV).

By the end of Exodus 10, a stand-off exists between Pharaoh and Moses. The eighth plague of devouring locusts has brought devastation to the land of Egypt. The ninth plague has plunged the people into dense and terrifying darkness. Pharaoh remains unrepentant. Moses has nothing more to say.

God is ready to move centre stage. He tells Moses that, with the tenth plague, he will bring about an amazing reversal of all that Moses has seen and heard to this point.

- Pharaoh will not just let the people go, but will drive them out.
- The Israelite people, treated until now as cheap labour, will be showered by their Egyptian neighbours with gifts of silver and gold.
- Moses himself, once rejected, will be elevated to the place of highest esteem.

In the midst of this most dreadful and devastating plague, however, the Israelite people will be spared.

'Then you will know that the LORD makes a distinction between Egypt and Israel' (11:7). This phrase has echoed through most of the previous plagues. The plagues of flies and hail caused great damage to the land, but not Goshen, where the Israelites lived. The plague which brought death to Egypt's livestock spared the animals of the Israelites. The darkness of the ninth plague did not extinguish the light over the Israelites. And so it went on.

Each plague had brought devastation to all, except God's people. While judging Egypt, God shows that he can and will preserve his people. In a most dramatic way, the last plague will confirm that distinction for all time.

The Israelite people may not yet understand why they are being spared, but later, in the desert, God will teach them the laws, principles and values that will make them distinct as his people for ever.

To reflect on
What makes you distinct as a person of God?

WEDNESDAY 8 AUGUST
The Lord's Passover

Exodus 12:1–36

'At midnight the LORD struck down all the firstborn in Egypt, from the firstborn of Pharaoh, who sat on the throne, to the firstborn of the prisoner, who was in the dungeon . . .' (v. 29, NIV).

We stand on holy ground as we read this account of the Lord's Passover. This is the story of redemption. It is both the narrative of what happened on that dark night, and the setting of a ritual by which the deliverance of the Hebrew people will be commemorated for all time. God said, 'This month is to be... the first month' (12:2). This great redemptive act was a new beginning for God's people.

The Passover began with an unblemished lamb, carefully chosen and guarded, until the designated moment of slaughter. The blood was then smeared on the doorframes of their houses, thus marking them as Israelite. Inside their homes, the people ate a meal of roast lamb, unleavened bread and bitter herbs. The bread could be made quickly, because the dough did not have to rise. Bitter herbs signified the bitterness of slavery. The meal was to be eaten in haste. Dressed in travelling clothes (12:11), the Hebrews were to be ready to leave at any moment. They were not yet free, but were to prepare themselves for freedom, for God had spoken!

And so God moved throughout the land. That night, the first-born son of every family who did not have blood on the doorposts was killed. Every Egyptian family, from the exalted Pharaoh to the lowest prisoner in jail, was affected. The agonising cry of loss throughout the land of Egypt was met with the sounds of silence among the Israelites in Goshen (11:7). Pharaoh surrendered and commanded Moses to 'just go, *go*, GO!' The slave people, now free, were driven out, laden with gifts from the Egyptians glad to be rid of them. Yahweh, 'I AM', revealed to Moses back in the Midian desert, had proved to all – even Pharaoh who now asks for a blessing (12:32) – just who he is.

To reflect on
Jesus, our Passover Lamb (1 Cor 5:7) has been sacrificed for us. We are a redeemed people!

THURSDAY 9 AUGUST
A Night of 'Keepings'

Exodus 12:37–42; 13:11–16

'Because the LORD kept vigil that night to bring them out of Egypt, on this night all the Israelites are to keep vigil to honour the LORD for the generations to come' (12:42, NIV).

The exodus of the people of Israel from the land of Egypt was long awaited by Israel, much postponed by Pharaoh but carefully prepared and executed exactly on schedule by God. 'At the end of the 430 years, to the very day, all the Lord's divisions left Egypt' (*12:41*).

The abrupt departure – with kneading bowls in hand to make bread on the journey – after such a lengthy residence in the land, was according to God's perfect timetable. It was a night of 'keepings', a night when he kept his promises of release and protection, freedom and movement of his multiplied people toward the land he had promised them. In response, the Israelites were to make that a night of 'keepings' for God, a night when they would keep their promises of remembrance, generation after generation. What God did that night in Egypt he did for all Israel, in every generation.

As God had spared the first-born sons of the Israelite people, now he spoke of his rightful claim to the first-born, child and animal, not as a dead sacrifice, but as a living offering. The eating of unleavened bread, the offering of the first-born, and the ritual of telling the Passover story would keep the testimony of God's redemption alive for generations to come. Whatever they may become in the better times ahead, the people of Israel are never to forget what they were.

And so the people moved forward and out into freedom – thousands upon thousands of them, led forth during the day by a pillar of cloud and at night by a pillar of fire. The God who had kept and protected them in Egypt now goes before them in a visible symbol of his presence.

Praise
He has brought us this far by his grace.
He has led us by fire and by cloud.
He will bring us to Zion to look on his face.
O blessed, O blessed be God.
(Bonnie Low)

FRIDAY 10 AUGUST
The Victory Belongs to God Alone!

Exodus 14:1–31

'The LORD will fight for you; you need only to be still' (v. 14, NIV).

Recovering from the terrible tragedy that has affected himself and his people, Pharaoh hears that the Israelites are wandering aimlessly about, not knowing where to turn. As the shock of grief is replaced by practical considerations, he sees his opportunity to pursue and recapture his lost labour force, not knowing that God is luring him into a trap. He has his chariot prepared and gathers his elite fighting men and the larger chariot force under the command of his officers.

The people of Israel, unaware of the gathering threat, are moving forward in growing confidence and high spirits. They are three days' journey away by now. They have been delivered. The bondage of slavery has been broken. God is with them. The sun is shining and all is well with the world. But, as they lift their eyes, they see clouds of dust from pursuing chariots, bearing down upon them. In despair and panic, they cry out to God and protest to Moses.

Moses is unruffled. He has obviously seen too much of God's deliverance to be afraid now. He ignores their sarcastic attack on his leadership and commands them to set fear aside, to stand firm where they are, and to see how God will save them. The Egyptians, whom they now see with such terror, they will soon see no more. God is going to fight this battle for them. They have only to be still.

There is a time to pray and a time to move. There is no obvious way of escape, but God opens up a dry path through the sea. As they move forward, the pillar of cloud that has guided them by day now moves behind the company, blocking the pursuing Egyptians from view. At the decisive moment, in the light of a new day when all can see, God lets the walls of water fall and the sea returns to its place, drowning the pursuers. The waters that have allowed Israel's escape are now the waters of Egypt's destruction.

To reflect on
This victory belongs to God alone!

SATURDAY 11 AUGUST
A Song of Deliverance

Exodus 15:1–21

'The LORD is my strength and my song; he has become my salvation' (v. 2, NIV).

God has rescued his people as he had promised. He must be praised – and praised he is. The divine name Yahweh ('the LORD') appears ten times in these verses. He is both the subject and object of this hymn – it is both about him and to him. With one voice the whole community praises God. They look back and retell the story of the deliverance at the Red Sea *(vv. 1–12)*; they look forward, anticipating his power and love as they approach the land of Canaan *(vv. 13–18)*.

God is praised as a 'man of battle', a 'warrior'. Pharaoh's entire military force offered no threat to such a God. He threw them into the sea, as a fisherman would toss overboard the remains of the catch for seabirds to eat. The wind that moved the sea waters out of their channel (see *14:21*) is described as the wind of God's anger blowing through his nostrils *(v. 8)*, like an enraged bull about to charge.

The arrogant claims of the enemy, 'I will pursue, I will overtake, I will divide, I will gorge, I will draw my sword, my hand will destroy' *(v. 9)* are ridiculed as futile. God had merely to blow with his wind, and they were all covered, sinking like lead into the mighty waters.

God is thus extolled as incomparable among the gods. Even among the mighty divinities of Egypt there is simply none like God. His magnificent holiness, his praiseworthy deeds, his extraordinary accomplishments, set him apart from all others *(v. 11)*.

The second part of this song *(vv. 13–18)*, no doubt written later, keeps the same theme – praise of the incomparable God, whose saving presence rescues, protects and establishes his people. The song as a whole celebrates God, present with his people and doing for them what no other god anywhere at any time can ever do.

Today
Lift your heart in praise to this wonder-working God, thanking him for the deliverance he has worked in your life.

SUNDAY 12 AUGUST
A Prayer about Words

Psalm 12

'The words of the LORD are flawless, like silver refined in a furnace of clay, purified seven times' (v. 6, NIV).

The young woman's accusations hit me like a slap on the face. She had come to me in distress, and I listened and gently encouraged her. We looked at her options, then prayed together before she left. Now here she was, just a few days later, telling people I had told her what she must do. She had reported the options as orders! I felt devastated as lies were told, and believed by others. I knew that day what the author of Psalm 12 felt as he wrote his despairing words. 'Help, Lord,' was all I could pray.

The psalmist must have felt as if he were drowning in a sea of words. Lies, flattery, boasting swirled all around him. Good people seemed to have disappeared, but the wicked were everywhere. He sounds like Elijah who, in his time of testing, felt that he was the only upright person left alive (1 Kgs 19:10).

The evil that he lamented is the evil of lies, flattery, boasts, fine-sounding words that contain no substance. These sharp weapons, every bit as deadly as swords, threatened the lives of the innocent. The greatest crime of the evil-speakers was pride. 'Who is our master?' they asked, believing that the answer was 'No one!' Arrogantly refusing to acknowledge the mastery of God, they oppressed the servants of God with their tongues.

Halfway through the psalm, a change in the psalmist's tone indicates a change in his perspective. The deadly words of the wicked (v. 5) are contrasted with the life-giving words of God. 'I will now arise, I will protect them,' says God. His words are flawless and pure, refined like silver, a most precious metal, in contrast with the words of the evil ones, which are filled with the dross of flattery and vanity. The wicked still strut about, their speech is still vile, but God's word will protect his children (v. 7). That's God's promise to us today.

To reflect on
If you are suffering from the lash of spiteful words, don't retaliate, but refer your case to God.

MONDAY 13 AUGUST
Petulance and Provision

Exodus 16:1–21

'I have heard the grumbling . . . At twilight you will eat meat, and in the morning you will be filled with bread. Then you will know that I am the LORD your God' (v. 11, NIV).

The full-hearted singing of praise has scarcely stopped when a new sound emerges from the people of Israel, a bitter resentful complaining at the lack of water, meat and bread in the wilderness. Is this really the same people who were so recently singing their songs of deliverance? Does God not lose patience, having to prove to them yet again that he is the Lord, and able to provide? Would we be any different, in similar circumstances? After all, water is a matter of life and death, especially in the dehydrating heat of the desert.

The wilderness of Sin (it seems aptly named, although is probably derived from 'Sinai') was a wasteland, a hostile environment of sand and stone. The barren surroundings provided the perfect place for God to test and shape the character of his people. Having taken the people out of Egypt, God now has to take Egypt out of them!

The panic of thirst is changed to the contentment of provision (15:24,25). God uses this 'teachable moment' to establish their options and his promises. 'If you . . . then I will' (15:26). Such testing will be repeated time and time again. Blessing will result from their obedience, punishment will be the consequence of their disobedience. God provides, purifying the polluted water and guiding them to an oasis overflowing with both water and fruit (15:27).

Six weeks later (16:1) Israel has moved on, settling into a routine. The newness of freedom has worn off, the hardship of wilderness life has set in, and they complain again to Moses, but really to God. Fantasising about the good life and abundant diet back in Egypt, they cry out for meat and bread. God patiently responds, providing quail at night and fresh white flakes of honeydew in the morning. This miraculous provision, as always, comes with a test (16:4) which, sad to say, is not passed by everybody (16:20).

To reflect on
Jesus is our bread of life, day by day by day (John 6:48).

TUESDAY 14 AUGUST
A Wise Father-in-Law

Exodus 18:1–27

'Now I know that the LORD is greater than all other gods, for he did this to those who had treated Israel arrogantly' (v. 11, NIV).

A wise figure now steps centre stage – Jethro, Moses' father-in-law, who has not been mentioned since the days when Moses lived in Midian. He comes, on God's cue, with a word of wisdom for Moses.

On hearing of God's mighty acts in Egypt, Jethro praises God for what he has done. This Midianite has understood the lesson of the Exodus in a way that neither the Egyptians nor the Amalekites (*chapter 17*) were able to grasp: 'The LORD is greater than all other gods.' God had said that his dealings with Pharaoh were so that 'my name might be proclaimed in all the earth' (*9:16*). Jethro understands that and gives the proper response – praise.

Moses had referred to 'sacrifice in the desert' in his earlier dealings with Pharaoh (*3:18; 5:3; 8:27*). This fellowship meal with his father-in-law in Moses' tent is the first of many such occasions. The characters who sit at this meal symbolise God's gracious workings in the life of his people. Moses belonged to Israel by birth and to Midian by marriage. As he sits with Jethro and the elders of Israel he becomes a bridge linking the two parts of the family separated by strife and jealousy since Abraham's day (see *Gen 25:1–6*).

Jethro is a practical man and obviously a skilled organiser. He sees the overwhelming demands being placed on Moses as people come to him to seek God's will in the settling of their disputes. Jethro suggests a solution to ease the burden on Moses by increasing the number of judges. This works well for the time being but, within a few chapters, another solution will be presented. Rather than needing to consult Moses or a judge, at Mount Sinai the people themselves will become directly aware of what God requires of them (*chapters 20–23*). The goal to which God stretches his people in every age is to have his law written on their hearts.

To reflect on
Is God's law written on your heart?

WEDNESDAY 15 AUGUST
Return to Sinai

Exodus 19:1–15

'Although the whole earth is mine, you will be for me a kingdom of priests and a holy nation' (vv. 5,6, NIV).

Moses comes again to Mount Sinai where he had earlier encountered God in the burning bush. This time he brings a whole nation with him. The events that are about to take place are the climax of the Exodus story, the supreme act of God towards which everything else has been moving. Having liberated the people of Israel from slavery, God is now about to establish for ever just who he is, who they are, and what their relationship with him is to be.

God calls to Moses from the mountain and summarises what he has done for the people. They have seen for themselves 'what I did to Egypt', from the first of the mighty acts to the deliverance at the Red Sea. They have experienced him carrying them 'on eagles' wings' in his guidance and provision in the desert. Now he has brought them to himself, to the mountain of his special presence.

'Now if . . .' (v. 5) – God does not force them to serve him as some conquering king might do, but offers them a choice, just as Joshua will say to the people later, 'Choose for yourselves this day . . .' (Josh 24:15). God makes clear what the results of their choosing will be.

Israel's positive response will first of all mean the birth of the people of Israel as God's own, unique 'special treasure'. They will be his prized masterwork, a kingdom of priests, a holy nation. They will show to all the world what it means to be a people of faith living in covenant relationship with God. The covenant made with Abraham 600 years earlier (Gen 17) is now restated to Abraham's promised descendants.

Moses relays God's message and the people respond affirmatively, promising to obey the terms of the covenant. Moses instructs them to prepare themselves for holiness. Outward preparation symbolises inner consecration. Until now the people have heard about God through Moses. Now, with trembling anticipation, they prepare to meet him for themselves.

To reflect on
Six hundred years, maybe, but still . . . 'The Lord is not slow in keeping his promise' (2 Pet 3:9).

THURSDAY 16 AUGUST
The Ten Commandments

Exodus 20:1–17

'I am the LORD your God, who brought you out of Egypt, out of the land of slavery' (v. 1, NIV).

God comes at daybreak on the third day (*19:16*). He comes with thunder, lightning, heavy cloud, fire, smoke and the resounding ram's horn, to his people, gathered by his instruction at the edge of a boundary set for their protection. His coming is dramatic; his words even more so.

He reminds them first of all of who he is – the God 'who brought you out of Egypt, out of the land of slavery'. His words leave them in no doubt as to who they are – liberated slaves who owe their freedom and their very existence to God. This first verse introduces the Ten Commandments, a series of principles which will govern their relationship with God and with all mankind.

From a people who have recently come from a culture filled with deities and idols, God demands an exclusive one-to-one relationship, an undivided loyalty. This commandment is the foundation of the covenant. As God has given himself in unique relationship to Israel, the relationship can develop only if, in return, the people pledge themselves in unique relationship to God.

The next three commandments give specifications on how God is to be worshipped – without the use of images to represent him, by honouring his name, and by setting apart the Sabbath as a day for holy purposes.

The next six commandments set out the guiding principles of living in community with others. Parents, the channel of God's gift of life and the starting point for every human relationship, are to be honoured. Murder, adultery, stealing, perjury and lust are all prohibited.

The order of the commandments is significant, as it moves from Israel's first priority – God – to Israel's second priority – family and neighbour, to all men and women everywhere. This is what it means to be a people called by God.

To reflect on
'You shall have no higher priority in life than God.' What is the challenge of this first commandment for you today?

FRIDAY 17 AUGUST
The Covenant Confirmed

Exodus 24:1–18

'When Moses went and told the people all the LORD's words and laws, they responded with one voice, "Everything the LORD has said we will do" ' (v. 3, NIV).

The Ten Commandments have been given by God at Sinai. They must now be applied to the everyday lives of God's people. Authentic religion is always more than an initial, dazzling encounter; it must be lived out in practice day by day.

The guidelines for living spelt out in the next few chapters (21–23) require goodness and justice in all areas of community life – humane treatment of slaves, response to personal injuries, respecting others' rights, the valuing of children, responsible care of animals, restitution, social responsibility to the powerless, protection for the poor, justice and respect for all human beings. These covenant laws are the marks of a truly alternative society, for at the heart of them all is relationship with God. His words echo through every instruction: 'I am your God. You are my people.' All of life is to be an act of worship.

Guidelines are then given regarding Sabbath laws and the keeping of three yearly festivals which will celebrate God's mighty works and provision for his people.

The people hear God's laws and promise to obey. There follows a promise of the conquest of Canaan (23:20) which they are about to enter, and a solemn ritual of ratification (24:4). Moses builds an altar and offers the largest and costliest of animals as sacrifice. The blood is drained off, half of it is sprinkled over the altar to show that a sacrifice has been made, and the other half is sprinkled on the people as a sign that their sins have been dealt with. 'This is the blood of the covenant', says Moses (v. 8), words that Jesus himself will personalise (Matt 26:28).

The leaders have seen God (vv. 9,10); the people feel his holiness upon their very clothing and faces. They respond, 'We will do everything the LORD has said; we will obey.' By entering into a covenant sealed in blood, the people bind themselves to God forever.

A prayer
I bind myself to him today
In covenanted grace.
His plan made known, His call I own
I now His will embrace.

(Harry Read)

SATURDAY 18 AUGUST

Mayhem and Mercy

Exodus 33:1–23; 34:29–35

'The LORD replied, "My Presence will go with you, and I will give you rest" ' (33:14, NIV).

If only the story of Exodus could close at the end of chapter 24! God is with his people; Moses is on the mountain in communion with him; the people are forgiven and full of holy resolve.

But Moses is delayed and the people, not unnaturally, become unsettled. With Moses absent, their access to God is cut off, so they go to Aaron and ask him to 'produce' God, as Moses had done. Aaron complies, fashioning a calf from Egyptian gold. This do-it-yourself god is an idol, a direct violation of the second commandment.

Angry at their blatant disobedience, God tells Moses he is going to destroy them. Moses pleads for the people God has so recently liberated. He knows God's heart well enough to be sure that God will not destroy what he has saved. And so God relents (32:14).

Moses descends, sees the revelry for himself, hears Aaron's absurd explanation and in outrage shatters the tablets and destroys the calf. He invites those who are on God's side to separate themselves, and these loyalists slaughter the calf-worshippers.

God instructs Moses to go forward into Canaan, guided by his messenger, but God himself will not go with them. At this dreadful news the people plunge into mourning. Without his presence, what will become of Israel? Moses pleads once again, reminding God that unless he goes with them, their identity as a holy nation – God's special treasure – and all that has so recently been promised, will be lost.

God responds graciously, promising his presence, but Moses asks for assurance. He calls Moses up the mountain again and there the two meet as friends. God reveals his name and his nature – compassion, grace, love, faithfulness, forgiveness. Before the face of God, Moses worships. With the provision of two new stone tablets, the covenant requirements are restated and the shattered relationship restored. Moses descends the mountain, this time to awe and acceptance, his face aglow with the glory of God.

To reflect on
Who are you, Lord? Compassion, grace, love, faithfulness, forgiveness.

SUNDAY 19 AUGUST
May the Lord Make His Face Shine upon You

Psalm 13

'But I trust in your unfailing love; my heart rejoices in your salvation' (v. 5, NIV).

Psalm 13 is an anguished complaint concerning a prolonged illness. The sickness is bad enough, but worse, the psalmist wonders why God has hidden his face. He knows the grey despair of God's absence and begs him to make his presence known.

Everything seems bleak. Forgotten, abandoned, tormented, these feelings are bad enough, but he is afraid as well. The psalmist knows that death would mean a final separation from God. That would be the greatest bitterness of all. So he prays for deliverance from Enemy Death and from the exultation of evil people that would greet the news of his death (v. 4).

He implores God with his desperate cries: 'Look on me.' 'Turn your face towards me, look at me again, remember me and the covenant of love you made with your people.' 'Answer me.' That is, answer the fourfold question 'How long?' of the opening verses. 'Give light to my eyes.' The eyes are a window into the vitality of the body, and it is obvious that the psalmist's eyes have long since lost their sparkle.

This is more than a prayer for physical health. At a deeper level, he desires to return to close fellowship with God. For the psalmist, the essence of life is a relationship with God. That is why both the body and soul exist. In turning to him and looking upon him, God would bring healing to their relationship.

In his present afflicted state, he remembers God's unfailing love in the past, the faithful covenant love which has characterised all God's dealings with his chosen people. That is enough to help him accept the present, and to give hope for the future. This is no sudden miraculous healing; rather, a calm and confident anticipation of God's blessing and deliverance. When God withholds his hand, the psalmist knows he can trust his heart.

To reflect on
*The L*ORD *bless you and keep you;*
*the L*ORD *make his face shine upon you*
 and be gracious to you;
*the L*ORD *turn his face toward you*
 and give you peace.'

(Num 6:24–26)

LORD, TEACH US TO PRAY

Introduction

If we want to learn how to pray, our beginning point must be Jesus. When Jesus lived on earth, he taught people to pray, not by running seminars on the topic, or interactive workshops, but by being caught in the act.

And so he prayed – on dark, early morning hillsides, in quiet gardens and by freshly occupied tombs, in solitude and in crowds. He prayed before difficult decisions and when the pressure of his work was heaviest. Prayer was life for Jesus, as natural as breathing, for it was the language of his relationship with his Father. He made no apology for praying, but made it such a priority that others wanted to know how to pray as he did. In responding to their request, 'Teach us to pray', he gave them a pattern that today we call the Lord's Prayer.

This wonderful prayer is familiar to many Christians, and is recited in many churches and homes every day of the week. There's a great deal more that could be said about prayer, but this is a good place to begin. And if this was the only prayer we ever prayed, it would be enough, for it covers every aspect of our relationship with God and with each other. Having learned how to pray it, we are then called to live it.

Over the next two weeks we are going to slow the pace of this prayer and examine it in close detail. So come, let yourself be still, think of those for whom you want to pray, and gather them all up in the word 'Our'. Jesus is about to teach us how to pray.

MONDAY 20 AUGUST
Lord, Teach Us to Pray

Luke 11:1–4

'Lord, teach us to pray' (v. 1, NIV).

Jesus was a man of prayer. He lived among people for whom prayer was part of everyday life. The historian Josephus wrote, 'Twice each day, at its beginning and when the hour of sleep approaches, it is fitting to remember in gratitude before God the gifts which he gave us after the deliverance from Egypt.'

From the age of twelve, all Jewish males would recite the *Shema*, a series of texts from Torah, beginning with Deuteronomy 6:4: 'Hear (Hebrew: *Shema*), O Israel: the LORD our God, the LORD is one.' The reciting of this and other key texts would be a reminder of God's great saving acts in the life of the nation. It would also be a powerful means of passing on the tradition of prayer to the next generation. Israelite parents were told to 'Fix these words of mine in your hearts and minds ... Teach them to your children, talking about them when you sit at home and when you walk along the road, when you lie down and when you get up' (*Deut 11:18,19*).

Thus prayer was as natural as breathing, eating, sleeping. It filled every part of day and night, touching every activity of life with the fragrance of God's goodness and covenant love. Into such a prayer-filled atmosphere the human Jesus came and grew. He took on the discipline of prayer for himself. But when we look at Jesus at prayer, there is a dimension deeper than mere discipline. This is a man for whom prayer is life itself. He spoke of his relationship with God as food – meat and drink, basic essentials without which he could not exist (see *John 4:32*).

His disciples also recognised this. When they came asking him to teach them to pray, they weren't asking for words – they would already know the texts to recite. But they saw in Jesus an intimacy with the Father that they too wanted. And so their question.

Prayer
Lord Jesus, I too long for an intimacy of relationship with the Father.
Please teach me how to live in God's presence, as you did.

TUESDAY 21 AUGUST
A Time to Pray

Luke 4:42–44

'Pray in the Spirit on all occasions with all kinds of prayers and requests . . . be alert and always keep on praying'

(Ephesians 6:18, NIV).

Jesus had not only *time* for prayer, but also *a time* for prayer. Mark tells us that he got up 'very early in the morning, while it was still dark' (*Mark 1:35*). Luke says, 'at daybreak' (*Luke 4:42*).

I can almost hear a groan echo around the world as those who do not see themselves as 'morning people' read these words. Some people sparkle with bright eyes and a clear head in the fresh hours of the new day, then collapse in the early evening. Others take several hours and doses of black coffee to get going in the morning, and then want to party all evening! It's called the 'lark and owl syndrome'.

Jesus's pattern of prayer was more than a personality preference. It was an expression of his utter dependence upon God. The glimpses we have of him at prayer suggest that he prayed regularly, during the hours of the night or in the early morning. Perhaps those were the only times when he could be on his own, away from the demands of people. Certainly he prayed before the momentous decisions he faced, such as the choosing of the twelve who would become his specially commissioned apostles (*Luke 6:12,13*), and in Gethsemane, as he agonised over the cross that towered darkly above him (*Mark 14:32ff.*).

One gets the impression that when Jesus prayed, he was not only enjoying the intimacy of his relationship with the Father but he was also getting his orders for the day. He knew with certainty that his very purpose for living was to do the Father's will, and that will seems to have been revealed to him step by step, day by day, prayer by prayer, just as it is for us.

Like a fisherman setting out in his boat in the darkness of the pre-dawn, he sought the Father's blessing upon the work and the journey of the day. We are invited to do the same.

To reflect on
'Hurry is the death of prayer.'
(St Teresa)

WEDNESDAY 22 AUGUST
'Make in My Heart a Quiet Place'

Matthew 6:5–6

'When you pray, go into your room, close the door and pray to your Father, who is unseen . . .' (v. 6, NIV).

If we are to follow the pattern of Jesus, there is both a time for prayer, and a place. He himself sought uninterrupted quiet, an undisturbed place, away from the relentless demands of people (see *Mark 1:35*).

He had firm words for those who deliberately prayed in open, public places, in the synagogues and on the corners of the main roads (see *Matt 6:1,5,6*). For those who wanted to be seen as 'holy', public prayer was one way to get attention. Jesus saw right through such self-righteousness and taught that the heart of prayer is not public show but private communion. He made it clear that a true reward for prayer will come only when prayer is directed to God, is genuine, and is not to impress others. And so he recommended a private prayer place with a door that could be shut.

Such a private place may be a luxury or even an impossibility for many people. Those living in a crowded or confined physical situation may have no solitary place to slip away to. Others may not have the emotional freedom to withdraw for prayer.

Susanna Wesley, mother of John and Charles and seventeen other children, is reported to have found her prayer place – under her apron! When the children saw their mother with her apron thrown up over her face, they knew she was at prayer, and not to be disturbed.

A modern-day woman of prayer said that her husband would not be happy to know she is praying, so she closes her eyes during the commercial breaks on TV, and he thinks she is dozing! Many prayers use a special chair in a corner for prayer, or a seat out in the garden. I have a friend for whom the local park with its lush trees is a cathedral.

To reflect on
'Even when I am denied a space to be quiet with you, there is still a space inside me, Lord, an inner room where you are waiting for me, and which I can enter at any moment.'

(Angela Ashwin,
Patterns Not Padlocks)

THURSDAY 23 AUGUST
Words and No Words

Matthew 6:5–8

'And when you pray, do not keep on babbling like pagans . . .
for your Father knows what you need before you ask him'
(vv. 7,8, NIV).

A woman came regularly to a prayer group, but seldom prayed out loud. She was a 'rough diamond' sort of person, but the fact that she attended week after week suggested an inner sensitivity to the things of God. One day she came, worried about a family matter, and burst out in prayer, 'Lord, I don't know how to pray about this, so I just want to gather it all up and put it in your lap!'

That's the kind of prayer that Jesus would welcome. He had harsh words for those who piled up meaningless words. 'Babbling like pagans', he described it, the repetition of the same words over and over like a magic incantation, or the chanting of long lists of the names of their gods, in the hope that one or other of them would help. Jesus condemned this shallow repetition of words that are not offered with a sincere heart. 'You don't have to pray like that,' he told his followers, 'for God knows what you need even before you ask.'

Some have questioned the need for prayer when God knows the need anyway. He is like a father, who delights to hear his children bring their requests before him and 'lay them in his lap'. And so our words of request are welcome, as they express our trust in God's great ability to hear and answer.

There are times, however, when words fail us and we do not know 'what we ought to pray for' (*Rom 8:26*). A loved one is ill; a crisis has occurred; the TV news brings horrific pictures from some troubled part of the world. In such moments, says Paul, we are to trust the Spirit to interpret our needs and to intercede on our behalf.

To reflect on
Whether your prayer today is with words, or in a wordless expression of the heart, be confident that God knows what you need!

FRIDAY 24 AUGUST
'Our Father in Heaven'

Matthew 6:9–13

'This, then, is how you should pray: "Our Father in heaven . . ."'
(v. 9, NIV).

Having dealt with the time and place of prayer, and the matter of words, Jesus now teaches his followers a pattern for prayer that is one of the enduring texts of the Scriptures. The whole of what we call the Lord's Prayer is really a meditation on the two opening words – 'Our Father'. The first part of the prayer outlines what the Father expects of his children – reverence, loyalty, obedience. The second part says what the children may expect of the Father – provision, pardon, protection.

The word *Abba*, translated 'Daddy', is the delightful expression that Jesus used in addressing God. It is a name that speaks of the affection, trust and joy of an intimate relationship with God and, at the same time, reverence and awe, for he is 'in heaven'. As Father, God is concerned for the needs of his children; as the one in heaven, he is all-powerful!

A biblical scholar told of an occasion when he was flying in the Middle East. Coming down the steps of the plane alongside a Palestinian father, he heard a little boy at the bottom of the steps shouting delightedly to his father, 'Abba! Abba!' The scholar commented, 'That is exactly the feel of "Abba" in the New Testament.'

We too are invited to call him by this name, and we can do so

- gratefully, because of what Christ has done on our behalf;
- reverently, because God is 'in heaven'; and
- unselfishly, because God is *our* Father.

To reflect on

Our image of God, how we picture or think of him, determines our relationship with him, which in turn determines our prayer. Choose a new name for God today – 'Abba, Father, Mother, Lover, Friend, Companion, Shepherd, Helper, Creator, Counsellor, Guide, Inspirer' – and lift your heart to him in prayer, with joy and reverence.

SATURDAY 25 AUGUST
'Hallowed Be Your Name'

Matthew 6:9–13

'I have made you known to them, and will continue to make you known in order that the love you have for me may be in them and that I myself may be in them' (John 17:26, NIV).

Many people speak the name of God, but in a careless, irreverent manner. Hitler used it a great deal. Insurance companies speak of 'acts of God' as though he is responsible for earthquakes and other 'natural' disasters. A child stumbling over this prayer says, 'Harold be your name.'

Martin Buber says the name of God is 'the most loaded word in any language'. It is a name that is trivialised, abused and misunderstood. But it is a name that Christians are called to hallow, keep holy, handle with care and reverence, as one would hold something precious in one's hands.

The name of God reveals his character, which was most clearly shown in the human Jesus. 'Anyone who has seen me has seen the Father,' he said (John 14:9). To hear Jesus at prayer is to learn a pattern for our own praying. To see him living is to have a model for our own lives. To glimpse the God whom he addressed, loved and honoured is to form a picture of what God can be like for us. Called to hallow his name, we are called to 'make it holy', 'set it apart', 'consecrate it'. It is for holy use, not for empty, careless or irreverent handling.

A retired Salvation Army officer I know worked for many years in his pre-Christian days as a sheep farmer. His most valuable assets were his keen-eyed sheepdogs. He had his own way of speaking to them, in a language that was full of expletives, but when he became a Christian, he had to get rid of his dogs, because they no longer responded to his new cleaned-up language!

Set apart – keep it holy – hallowed be your name!

To reflect on
Is it time for you to have a language check-up? How is the name of God in your heart and on your tongue?

SUNDAY 26 AUGUST
Are You a Fool?

Psalm 14

'The LORD looks down from heaven on the sons of men to see if there are any who understand, any who seek God' (v. 2, NIV).

Growing up on a sheep farm, and living in a country with about fifty million sheep, I've had plenty of opportunity to observe sheep at close quarters. While tourists flock to this country to admire these woolly creatures and to buy products made from their wool, the frank opinion of many New Zealanders is that sheep are stupid. My dogmatic opinion is based on seeing sheep follow each other. If you want to get a flock of sheep to go in one direction, you get one to go and the rest will follow. It's that childhood game of follow-the-leader – in woolly jackets!

Stupid, foolish – these are strong words to describe anything. It's a shock to read the start of Psalm 14 which makes an even more dogmatic statement. Fools in this context were not stupid people. In fact they were often intelligent, even wealthy and successful. But they were fools because they rejected God, living without any reference to a holy, covenant-making, covenant-keeping God. Their corrupt deeds gave proof of their foolishness.

Looking down from heaven, God had scanned the earth to see if he could locate any whom he could call 'wise', seekers after God. His conclusion seems to be that all humans appear to be corrupt. They (we!) are all fools, lacking knowledge and understanding, and bringing grief and oppression to others. Like sheep, people have gone astray, following-the-leader right into sin. Isaiah picked up this cry (*Isa 53:6*) and Paul repeated it (*Rom 3:10–12*).

The psalm ends on a note of rejoicing at the anticipation of deliverance (*v. 7*). But the serious challenge of the earlier verses remains. This psalm is not just about other people. Everyone who lives without reference to God is a fool, separated from his wisdom. The ultimate expression of God's wisdom is found in Jesus Christ. Sadly, many today still reject him as foolishness (see *1 Cor 1:23–25*).

To reflect on
When it comes to Jesus, the wisdom of God, are you a seeker, or a sheep?

MONDAY 27 AUGUST
'Your Kingdom Come'

Matthew 6:9–13

'This, then, is how you should pray: . . . your kingdom come'
(vv. 9,10, NIV).

The day is fast approaching when I shall have to get bifocal glasses. I've been putting it off, as they seem to be the ultimate surrender to degenerating eyesight and creeping old age! And yet, in my 'sensible' moments, I know it would be very helpful to be able to see what I am reading and, at the same time, recognise the person who is coming through the door towards me.

There is a sense in which Christians have to be bifocal. This is a practised state of one's inner perspective, and has nothing to do with physical eyesight. When we pray 'your kingdom come', there are always two perspectives which we have to keep in mind. The kingdom of God is both 'already here' and 'still coming'. It is both present and future. One author has written about 'life in the overlap', this 'now' time between the old and the new (Jean Darnall, *Life in the Overlap*, Lakeland, 1977).

Jesus told his disciples, 'The kingdom of God is within you' (*Luke 17:21*) but he also looked forward, saying 'I will not drink again of the fruit of the vine until the kingdom of God comes' (*Luke 22:18*).

The apostle Peter wrote of the ultimate future fulfilment of the kingdom: 'In keeping with his promise we are looking forward to a new heaven and a new earth, the home of righteousness' (*2 Pet 3:13*).

So when the disciples were told to pray 'your kingdom come', they were being encouraged to pray that what they saw beginning in the person and ministry of Jesus would be experienced in all its fullness. When we utter this phrase, we too are praying both for the advance of the kingdom of God here and now, and for the future consummation of God's great purposes in history.

This is no small request! As we pray and work and wait, let us 'live holy and godly lives as [we] look forward to the day of God and speed its coming' (*2 Pet 3:11,12*).

Prayer
Maranatha – 'Our Lord, come!'

TUESDAY 28 AUGUST
'Your Will Be Done'

Matthew 6:9–13

'This, then, is how you should pray: . . . your will be done on earth as it is in heaven' (vv. 9,10, NIV).

Four young men were preparing to leave for South America in response to God's calling. 'What shall we do when we get there?' they asked an older Christian. 'When you get there,' he said, 'drive two stakes into the ground, string a line between them, then hang yourselves out like a sheet on the line and let the Spirit of God blow you where he wills!'

Such a response to the will of God is at the heart of this portion of the Lord's Prayer. For some people, the will of God is shrouded in mystery, revealed only to those who are spiritual giants, willing to be missionaries or martyrs! For others, the will of God is to be ignored or avoided at all costs, because it has the power to overturn carefully laid personal plans. For still others, it raises a question, 'How do you know?'

'Your will be done' has an echo of Isaiah's response after his vision of the Lord in the temple: 'Here I am. Send me!' The word translated 'will' in the New Testament is dynamic, never merely passive. It means a fervent wish or longing. The writer to the Hebrews summed up the whole life and work of Jesus in the words of the psalmist, 'I have come to do your will, O God' (*Heb 10:7*). In all that he did, Jesus lived out his aim, which was 'not to please myself but him who sent me' (*John 5:30*).

God's will is wanting what God wants, not merely putting up with what God wants. Called to pray 'your will be done', we are to pray with our will, our intellect and our emotions, willing God's will out of trusting obedience, not reluctant resignation. Lord Tennyson wrote: 'Our wills are ours, we know not why; Our wills are ours to make them thine.'

To reflect on
When we pray 'your will be done', we must throw our lives after our prayer.

WEDNESDAY 29 AUGUST
Bread for Today

Matthew 6:9–13

'This, then, is how you should pray: . . . Give us today our daily bread' (vv. 9,11, NIV).

Our family arrived at Chikankata, Zambia, just before Easter 1975. With all the naivety of the uninitiated, I asked, 'Where can I buy Easter buns round here?' When my neighbour stopped laughing, she told me, 'You make them!'

So began my first lesson on missionary service! I discovered that there is something holy about making bread – the handling of the ingredients, the kneading, the waiting, the rising as the yeast does its miraculous work, the aroma which speaks warmth and welcome, and finally the sharing of the loaf with others. When we pray 'Give us today our daily bread', I long to pause and feel the dough in my hands and smell the bread baking. This is not a prayer for rushing through.

Bread is commonplace, ordinary, an everyday part of everyone's culture in one form or another. In praying these words, we declare our dependence on God's provision and our intention to live each day as it comes, trustfully, not worrying or anxious about coming days or the unknown future.

In praying 'Give us' we take our eyes off our own shopping list of needs and turn them onto the needs of others. While food is stockpiled in one country, and people in another starve to death, these words must continue to be prayed. Let us receive, and let us share with others not just the aroma of the loaf, but its substance.

Then, beyond the physical bread, we are reminded of Jesus who called himself the Bread of Life and promised that 'the person who aligns with me hungers no more and thirsts no more' (*John 6:35, The Message*). There is a soul emptiness that is greater than physical hunger. There is also nourishment and satisfaction that is not dependent on how much one has eaten.

To reflect on
'I have experienced union with the eternal. And so I possess a cordial which secures me from dying of thirst in the desert of life.'

(Albert Schweitzer)

THURSDAY 30 AUGUST
Forgiveness and Forgivingness

Matthew 6:9–15

'Be kind and compassionate to one another, forgiving each other, just as in Christ God forgave you' (Ephesians 4:32, NIV).

A story hit the local headlines recently of a car accident in which two children were killed by the careless driving of a young man. The two families lived close together in a suburban area, but were of different races. The case went to court and the young man was charged, but an appeal was made for his sentence to be reversed – by the family of the children who had been killed! In a costly act of reconciliation, and in a declaration of their Christian faith, the grieving family went to the family of the young man and extended their love and forgiveness to them. The story was widely publicised, with many people finding the notion of such forgiveness simply unbelievable.

The Lord's Prayer begins in heaven, but ends very much with its feet on the ground, in the fearsome phrase, 'Forgive us our debts, as we also have forgiven our debtors' (*Matt 6:12*). Literally it means, 'Forgive us our sins in proportion to the way we forgive those who have sinned against us.' Jesus says in the plainest possible language that only as we forgive others will God forgive us. Human forgiveness and divine forgivingness are woven together in such a way that they cannot be separated.

This prayer, with its emphasis on 'our', is a family prayer. It is to *our* Father we pray, asking for *our* daily bread, and now, most testing of all in a family, 'Father, forgive us as we forgive others.' Forgiveness releases us from having to get even with someone else for the hurt they have caused. It is not an end in itself, but a new beginning.

Prayer
Today, Lord, let me forgive. But if that is too big a step to take all at once, let me be willing for you to plant a seed of forgiveness in my heart that can grow and one day be offered to the one who has hurt me.

FRIDAY 31 AUGUST
Yield Not to Temptation

Matthew 6:9–15

'And lead us not into temptation, but deliver us from the evil one'
(v. 13, NIV).

I recall the relief of learning as a young Christian that temptation is a struggle for all believers, but that temptation in itself is not sin. I gratefully memorised the verse: 'No temptation has seized you except what is common to man. And God is faithful; he will not let you be tempted beyond what you can bear. But when you are tempted, he will also provide a way out so that you can stand up under it' (1 Cor 10:13).

The word translated 'temptation' is also translated 'testing'. 'To be tempted' is to be enticed to sin. 'To be tested' is to be brought into difficult circumstances that try one's faithfulness. The two are similar, since sin can result in either case, but they are also different. God does not lead into temptation (see *Jas 1:13*). He does, however, allow people to be tested so that faith can be strengthened (see *1 Pet 1:6,7*).

With the prayer 'Lead us not into temptation' we also pray 'but deliver us from the evil one'. As forgiven sinners we know all too well the power of evil, and so we pray, 'Rescue us, protect us against the evil forces that can easily trip us up. Help us to say "No" to evil and "Yes" to God.'

With this expression we return full circle, back to that simple dependence of children on God our Father. Our need for provision, pardon and protection can only be fully met in him. Jean-Pierre de Caussade said, 'In praying the Lord's Prayer we are to keep our gaze on our Father in heaven, and recognising our temptations, we are to look over their shoulder towards Jesus' (*Self-Abandonment to Divine Providence*).

The prayer concludes in many traditions with a doxology, a song of glory to God. *The Message* puts it in bold and colourful language:

You're in charge!
You can do anything you want!
You're ablaze in beauty!
Yes. Yes. Yes.

NOTES

1. Bill Gaither, copyright © William J. Gaither, Benson Company Inc., 365 Great Circle Road, Nashville, Tennessee 37228, USA
2. Brennan Manning, *The Signature of Jesus* (Multnomah Books, 1988)
3. Graham Kendrick, 'All I once held dear', copyright © 1993 Make Way Music, PO Box 263, Croydon, Surrey, CR9 5AP, UK. International copyright secured. All rights reserved. Used by permission.
4. C.S. Lewis, *Mere Christianity* (Fontana, 1960)
5. Tony Campolo, *The Kingdom of God is a Party* (Word, 1990)
6. Bonnie Low, copyright © 1976 Bonnie Low, 5B Redwing Street, Browns Bay, Auckland 10, New Zealand

INDEX
(as from: easter 1996)

Exodus		Pentecost 2001	John	11–12	Advent 1997
Joshua	5–10	Easter 1996		13–14	Easter 1998
	11–24	Pentecost 1996		14–15	Pentecost 1998
Judges	1–15	Advent 1996		15–17	Advent 1998
	15–21	Easter 1997		17	Easter 1999
Ruth	1–4	Easter 1997		17–18	Pentecost 1999
1 Samuel	1–4	Pentecost 1997		18–19	Advent 1999
	4–11	Advent 1997		19–20	Easter 2000
	12–15	Easter 1998		21	Pentecost 2000
	16–19	Pentecost 1998	1 Corinthians	1	Pentecost 1998
	20–28	Advent 1998		2–4	Advent 1998
	29–31	Easter 1999		5–10	Easter 1999
2 Samuel	1–6	Easter 1999		10–12	Pentecost 1999
	7–13	Pentecost 1999		12–13	Advent 1999
	13–20	Advent 1999		14–16	Easter 2000
	21–24	Easter 2000	2 Corinthians	1–6	Pentecost 2000
1 Kings	1–10	Easter 2000		7–11	Advent 2000
	11–18	Pentecost 2000		11–13	Easter 2001
	19–22	Advent 2000	Galatians	2–3	Easter 1996
2 Kings	2	Advent 2000		3–4	Pentecost 1996
	2–6	Easter 2001		4–5	Advent 1996
Psalms	1–14	Pentecost 2001		6	Easter 1997
Jeremiah	37–52	Easter 1996	1 Thessalonians	1	Easter 1997
The Disciples		Advent 1997		2–4	Pentecost 1997
Christ as pattern		Advent 1997		5	Advent 1997
Matthew	6	Pentecost 2001		5	Easter 1998
	20–25	Easter 1996	2 Thessalonians	1–2	Easter 1998
Mark	1	Pentecost 2000		3	Pentecost 1998
	1–3	Advent 2000	Hebrews	1–2	Advent 2000
	1–3	Pentecost 2001		3–4	Easter 2001
	4	Easter 2001	2 Peter	1	Easter 2001
John	6–7	Pentecost 1996	1 John		Pentecost 2001
	7–8	Advent 1996	Jude	vv.1–19	Pentecost 1996
	8–9	Easter 1997		vv.20–25	Advent 1996
	9–11	Pentecost 1997			

Words of Life Bible reading notes
are published three times a year:

Easter
(January–April)

Pentecost
(May–August)

Advent
(September–December)

In each edition you will find:

- informative commentary
- a wide variety of Bible passages
- topics for praise and prayer
- points to ponder
- cross references for further study

Why not place a regular order for *Words of Life*?
Collect each volume and build a lasting resource
for personal or group study.